LOVE LAYER CAKES

PEGGY PORSCHEN

Photography by Georgia Glynn Smith

QUADRILLE

Publishing Director Jane O'Shea
Commissioning Editor Lisa Pendreigh
Project Editor Katie Golsby
Creative Director Helen Lewis
Designer Gemma Hayden
Photographer Georgia Glynn Smith
Stylist Rebecca Newport
Production Director Vincent Smith
Production Controller Tom Moore

Props kindly provided by:
Talking Tables www.talkingtables.co.uk
India Jane www.indiajane.co.uk
Jane Means www.janemeans.com
Dotcomgiftshop www.dotcomgiftshop.com
Nina Campbell www.ninacampbell.com
Maids to Measure www.maidstomeasure.com

First published in 2015 by
Quadrille Publishing Ltd
Pentagon House, 52–54 Southwark Street,
London SE1 1UN
www.quadrille.co.uk

Quadrille is an imprint of Hardie Grant
www.hardiegrant.com.au

Text, recipes and cake designs
© 2015 Peggy Porschen
Photography
© 2015 Georgia Glynn Smith
Artwork, design and layout
© 2015 Quadrille Publishing Ltd

British Library Cataloguing-in-Publication Data
A catalogue record for this book is available
from the British Library

ISBN 978 1 84949 552 3

Printed in China

CONTENTS

INTRODUCTION

Love Layer Cakes is a book about two things I truly love: baking and creating beautiful, delicious cakes. I have loved cakes for as long as I can remember. I love looking at them, smelling them, eating them and, most of all, I love making them.

My love for cakes goes back to my very early childhood. Although people say that one's memories only go back to about the age of four, I still remember the moment of my very first birthday when my mum presented me with a lovely buttercream cake, covered in marzipan, with little sugar animals on top. (I have the photograph to prove it.) From that point, my birthday cake was the highlight of my year and, on my birthday, I always cared more about the cake than about my presents. I love how a cake brings people together around a table. A cake means a gathering of family and friends, it means happy moments and memories. So, what better way to celebrate a festive occasion than with a wonderful cake?

I was inspired to write *Love Layer Cakes* for all those reasons, and to combine creativity with delicious baking. At my home in Germany we have a similar saying to the English expression, 'You first eat with your eyes'. I have always cared about how a cake looks just as much as how it tastes. I meet a lot of people through my work who say that they can bake a delicious cake but, when it comes to the finishing touches, they struggle. The recipes in this book are about combining the most wonderful sponge cakes with delectable cake fillings and toppings that taste as good as they look. Some of the recipes are all-time classics, such as the Victoria sponge that is used as the base for the Citrus Cake (see pages 92–5) and the chocolate ganache that covers the Salted Caramel Cake (see pages 34–9), but I am always searching for the perfect version of any recipe so I often revisit them time and time again. Sometimes I use a classic recipe as the basis for a new flavour combination and add a new twist, such as in the Blueberry and Buttermilk Cake (see pages 18–21).

Before you start making any of the recipes in this book, I recommend that you carefully read through my top tips for baking the perfect sponge. If you follow the simple advice given here, you should avoid the disappointment of opening the oven to find that your sponge hasn't risen, or is burnt. The section on basic fillings and frostings offers a selection of recipes for buttercreams, frostings, ganache and sugar syrup, which you can flavour to your own taste and combine with the cake base of your choice. Towards the end of the book is a guide to layering and masking your cakes, with detailed step-by-step photography; I hope you will find this helpful, and that the advice given enables you to produce cakes that not only taste amazing, but also look worthy of the occasions that they are made for. For pretty finishing touches, there is a display of the different piping techniques that are used in the recipes. Finally, to help you to achieve simple yet effective cake decoration, I have designed two easy-to-use cake stencils that you will find tucked into the back of this book.

I hope you will *Love Layer Cakes* as much as I do.

Enjoy.

BASIC TOOL KITS

THE LISTS BELOW INCLUDE ALL THE TOOLS YOU WILL NEED TO CREATE THE LAYER CAKES IN THIS BOOK. IF YOU ARE ALREADY A KEEN HOME BAKER, YOU WILL PROBABLY HAVE IN YOUR KITCHEN MOST OF THE ITEMS LISTED IN THE BAKING TOOL KIT. THE LAYERING TOOLS ARE MORE SPECIFIC AND ARE A WORTHWHILE INVESTMENT TO ACHIEVE PERFECT RESULTS IF YOU WOULD LIKE TO TAKE YOUR CAKE-MAKING SKILLS TO THE NEXT LEVEL, AND THEY SHOULD SERVE YOU WELL FOR MANY YEARS TO COME.

BAKING TOOL KIT

1. Electric mixer with whisk and paddle attachment
2. Selection of cake tins and baking trays
3. Rubber spatula
4. Selection of bowls and jugs
5. Selection of large and small fine sieves
6. Kitchen scales
7. Greaseproof paper
8. Step palette knife
9. Pastry brush
10. Scissors
11. Wire cooling rack
12. Small kitchen knife
13. Whisk
14. Oven gloves
15. Measuring spoons
16. Cling film
17. Oil spray

LAYERING TOOL KIT

1. Long serrated knife or cake leveller
2. Ruler that measures in inches
3. Cake boards in various shapes and sizes
4. Small, medium and large palette knives
5. Non-slip turntable
6. Metal cake disc
7. Metal side scraper
8. Selection of piping bags (such as paper, plastic and textile with screw attachment)
9. Assortment of metal piping nozzles (different sizes of round and star nozzles)

Tucked inside the back cover of this book, you will find two food-safe stencils for decorating your layer cakes. For instructions on how to use these stencils, turn to pages 57–8. Made from food-safe plastic, these stencils can be used repeatedly. After each use, wash and dry the stencils. Wash the stencils by hand in warm soapy water and thoroughly dry them by laying them flat between sheets of paper towels and patting gently.

TOP TIPS FOR BAKING THE PERFECT SPONGE

BAKING MAY BE A SCIENCE BUT, IF YOU FOLLOW A FEW SIMPLE RULES, YOU WILL ACHIEVE CONSISTENTLY GOOD RESULTS AND EVENLY BAKED CAKES. HERE, I HAVE LISTED THE TIPS THAT I SWEAR BY WHEN IT COMES TO MAKING THE PERFECT SPONGE.

INGREDIENTS

1. Using good-quality ingredients really makes a difference, not only to the flavour but also to the bake. Always use free-range eggs, butter rather than margarine, and genuine spices, zests and extracts (not essences) where possible.

2. Unless otherwise stated, the eggs and butter should be the same temperature (room temperature is best) to prevent curdling, which will result in a low rise. For the same reason, always add the eggs gradually and beat well after each addition, until combined.

3. Bring the butter to room temperature before use, then cream together with the sugar until light and fluffy.

4. If a cake contains chopped fruits, biscuits or nuts, gently fold them in at the very end. To keep them from sinking to the bottom of the cake during baking, toss them with about one-quarter of the dry ingredients and gently fold them into the mixture.

5. It is important to use soft cake flour to achieve a good texture – don't be tempted to use a strong flour, such as bread flour, as it will make the sponge tough.

MEASUREMENTS

1. Use digital kitchen scales as opposed to traditional weighing scales, as they are much more precise. Weigh out your ingredients as accurately as possible and scrape out the bowls thoroughly.

2. Always use measuring spoons rather than a teaspoon or tablespoon from the cutlery drawer. Unless the recipe states otherwise, always level the top of the spoon with a knife.

3. Some of the recipes use medium eggs, some large – on average, the cracked weight of a medium egg is 50g and for a large egg it is 60g. If you have eggs of unequal sizes, calculate the total weight of egg needed, crack the eggs and weigh out the quantity required.

CAKE TINS

1. For light, evenly browned cakes, use shiny cake tins rather than dark or discoloured ones, as these will overbrown or even burn the cake.

2. I prefer to use a shallow sandwich tin for each layer (mine are 4cm deep), rather than one deep tin for the whole cake, as shallow sponges bake quicker, more evenly and rise better.

3. Spray the bottom and sides of the cake tin with oil and line the base with a disc of greaseproof paper.

4. Always spread the cake mix so it's a little higher around the edges than in the middle. This will prevent the sponge from 'erupting' in the centre.

5. Once filled, place the cake tins in a preheated oven as soon as possible; otherwise, the raising agent in the cake mix could lose its effect.

6. After baking, remove the sponges from the oven and leave to rest for 10 minutes. While still in the tin, brush with sugar syrup, using a pastry brush, and leave to rest for another 20–30 minutes until cool enough to handle. Run a small kitchen knife around the edges of the tins to release the sponges, then transfer to a wire cooling rack and leave to cool completely.

TIMING AND TEMPERATURES

1. Use any given timings and temperatures as a guide only, as ovens can vary greatly in their accuracy. The temperatures stated are for conventional ovens, so you will need to reduce the temperature by 20°C if using a fan-assisted oven.

2. A lot of domestic ovens have hot spots. If this applies to your oven, turn the cake tins halfway through cooking to ensure even baking.

BASIC FILLINGS AND FROSTINGS

THE CAKE FILLINGS AND FROSTINGS GIVEN HERE ARE USED THROUGHOUT THE BOOK. IT IS IMPORTANT TO ENSURE THAT YOU FOLLOW THE TIME PLAN GIVEN IN EACH CAKE RECIPE, SO THAT YOUR FILLING OR FROSTING IS THE REQUIRED TEMPERATURE AND CONSISTENCY AT THE TIME YOU NEED IT. THIS IS ESSENTIAL, TO GUARANTEE THAT THE CAKE HOLDS ITS SHAPE AND THAT THE OUTER COAT LOOKS SMOOTH AND NEAT. AS A GENERAL RULE, THE HEAVIER AND DENSER THE SPONGE, THE HEAVIER AND DENSER THE FROSTING SHOULD BE. HOWEVER, MY ADVICE IS TO EXPERIMENT AND USE WHATEVER WORKS BEST FOR YOU.

ENGLISH BUTTERCREAM

Making English buttercream is very straightforward; all you need is a good electric mixer. Made using just butter and icing sugar, the key to making it light and fluffy is beating it to incorporate as much air as possible. English buttercream doesn't split and holds up well, making it ideal for piped designs such as scrolls and rosettes. To make the buttercream stiffer – for example, on warm summer days – you can increase the amount of sugar up to double the amount of butter.

Makes 400g English buttercream
200g unsalted butter, softened
200g icing sugar, sifted
a pinch of salt

Place the butter, sugar, salt and any flavouring in the bowl of an electric mixer and, using a paddle attachment, beat at medium speed until light and fluffy.

If not using immediately, store the buttercream in a sealed container in the fridge and bring back to room temperature before use. It will keep for up to 2 weeks.

MERINGUE BUTTERCREAM

Meringue buttercream is very light and smooth with a relatively pale colour. It is more delicate than English buttercream and suits lighter sponges, such as chiffon cake. It can split easily if overworked or mixed with acidic ingredients or those with a high fat content, such as ganache. Always add other flavours very carefully, folding them through gently. Should the buttercream split, you can bring it back by whipping it at high speed (unless it is mixed with a filling containing a high fat content). Cakes filled with meringue buttercream should always be stored in the fridge because of the egg content.

Makes enough meringue buttercream to layer one 15cm cake
270g caster sugar
67ml water
135g egg whites, fresh or pasteurised
330g butter, softened

Place the sugar and water in a small saucepan over a medium-high heat and bring to a rapid boil.

Place the egg whites in the bowl of an electric mixer and whip at low speed, using the whisk attachment, until frothy.

When the sugar syrup reaches 121°C, with the mixer running, pour it directly over the meringue in a thin, steady stream. Take care not to pour any of the syrup onto the whisk or the sides of the bowl.

Whip the meringue until cool to the touch; this could take several minutes. With the mixer running, add the butter a couple of tablespoons at a time. Keep beating until the buttercream is completely smooth and spreadable, then fold in any additional flavourings.

Meringue buttercream will keep for up to 1 week in the fridge.

CREAM-CHEESE FROSTING

This is a scrumptious recipe that is perfectly coupled with many American-style cakes, such as the iconic Red Velvet Cake or Black and White Devil's Food Cake (see pages 60 and 68). It is softer than buttercream and needs to be refrigerated until serving.

Makes 1.125kg cream-cheese frosting
250g full-fat cream cheese, slightly softened
250g unsalted butter, softened
625g icing sugar, sifted

Place the cream cheese in a bowl and beat until smooth and creamy using an electric mixer.

Place the butter and a third of the sugar in a separate bowl and cream until very pale and fluffy. Add another third of the sugar and repeat.

Add the remaining sugar and beat again, scraping the sides of the bowl to ensure no lumps remain. Add the cream cheese, a little at a time, and mix at low speed until combined.

Chill until firm enough to spread or pipe.

Cream-cheese frosting will keep for up to 2 weeks in the fridge.

MASCARPONE FROSTING

This is a rich cake filling with a creamy texture. You must let it set properly before use, otherwise it won't hold up.

Makes 1kg mascarpone frosting
200g unsalted butter, softened
500g icing sugar, sifted
300g mascarpone, slightly softened

Place the butter and half of the sugar in the bowl of an electric mixer and cream together at high speed until very pale and fluffy.

Add the remaining sugar with the mascarpone and beat at medium-high speed, scraping down the sides of the bowl to ensure no lumps remain.

Beat until the mixture is smooth, but do not overbeat or the mixture will become runny. If necessary, chill until firm enough to pipe.

Chill for several hours until set completely.

Mascarpone frosting will keep for up to 2 weeks in the fridge.

CHOCOLATE GANACHE

This is a great basic ganache recipe with slightly less cream than chocolate, which allows it to set to just the right consistency for layering and masking cakes. The glucose adds a beautiful sheen, so it makes an ideal shiny chocolate glaze. For a perfect spreadable texture, leave the ganache to set slowly at room temperature.

Makes about 400g chocolate ganache
200g plain Belgian chocolate drops (53% cocoa solids)
150ml whipping cream
20g glucose

Place the chocolate drops in a deep bowl.

Pour the cream and glucose into a deep saucepan and bring to a simmer. *100 C° or 212 F°*

Pour the cream over the chocolate drops and whisk gently until the chocolate has melted and the mixture is smooth.

Leave to cool until just setting, before use. The ganache can be stored in an airtight container covered with cling film, and will keep for up to 2 weeks at room temperature.

SUGAR SYRUP

If you bake regularly at home, it's a good idea to keep a supply of simple sugar syrup in the fridge. I swear by it, as I use it to add moisture and flavour to most of my cakes. Brushing the top of a sponge with syrup just after baking prevents it from forming a dry, hard crust than can spoil the cake. Doing this while the sponge is still warm allows the syrup to absorb more quickly than if the sponge has cooled. For flavoured syrup, infuse the syrup with the flavouring as early as possible before use, to allow the flavours to develop fully.

Makes about 200ml sugar syrup
150ml water
150g sugar

Place the water and sugar in a saucepan, stir well and bring to the boil. Allow it to cool down.

When lukewarm, add the flavourings. Store the sugar syrup in the fridge if not using immediately. It will keep for up to 1 month.

RASPBERRY KISS CAKE

IF YOU WANT TO SAY IT WITH A CAKE, THEN THIS IS THE ONE FOR YOU. NOT ONLY IS IT MADE WITH LOVE, BUT IT ALSO TASTES TANTALISINGLY SWEET AND SCRUMPTIOUS. THE COMBINATION OF FRESH RASPBERRIES AND BITTERSWEET MELT-IN-THE-MOUTH CHOCOLATE IS A MATCH MADE IN HEAVEN. EVER WONDERED WHAT TO GIVE YOUR SWEETHEART FOR VALENTINE'S DAY? LOOK NO FURTHER.

INGREDIENTS

For the chocolate sponge
250ml sunflower oil
14 large eggs, separated
4 teaspoons vanilla extract
750g light brown sugar
400ml water
100g cocoa powder
600g plain flour
2 teaspoons bicarbonate of soda
1 teaspoon salt

For the chocolate ganache
400g plain Belgian chocolate drops (53% cocoa solids)
300ml whipping cream
40g glucose

For the meringue buttercream
540g caster sugar
135ml water
270g egg whites
660g butter

For the decoration
2–3 punnets of fresh raspberries

EQUIPMENT

baking tool kit (see page 8)
layering tool kit (see page 8)
three 20cm shallow heart-shaped cake tins
(or one deep tin – you will need to increase the baking time, then cut the sponge into 3 layers)
piping bag
sugar thermometer

Makes one 20cm heart-shaped cake, serving 10–12 generous slices.

METHOD

Make the sponge one day ahead.

TO MAKE THE CHOCOLATE SPONGE
Preheat the oven to 160°C/gas mark 3.

Line three 20cm heart-shaped cake tins with oil spray and greaseproof paper.

In a large bowl, using an electric mixer, blend the oil, egg yolks, vanilla extract, light brown sugar and water until well combined.

Sift the cocoa, flour, bicarbonate of soda and salt and gently fold into the mixture.

In a separate bowl, using an electric mixer, whisk the egg whites until they form stiff peaks. Fold into the batter and mix until everything is well combined.

Gently pour the mixture into the prepared tins and bake for 20–25 minutes. The sponges are cooked when they spring back to the touch and the sides are coming away from the edges of the tins. Alternatively, insert a clean knife into the middle of the sponge; if it is cooked, the knife will come out clean.

Once the sponges are baked, remove from the oven and allow them to rest for about 10 minutes.

Once just warm, run a knife all the way round the sides of the tins, transfer the sponges to a wire cooling rack and leave to cool completely.

Wrap the cooled sponges in cling film and leave them to rest overnight at room temperature. This will ensure that all the moisture is sealed and the sponges are the perfect firm texture for trimming and layering.

TO MAKE THE CHOCOLATE GANACHE
Please follow the instructions on page 13 using the amounts given on page 14.

TO MAKE THE MERINGUE BUTTERCREAM
Please follow the instructions on page 10 using the amounts given on page 14.

TO MAKE THE CHOCOLATE BUTTERCREAM
Check that the chocolate ganache and meringue buttercream are the same temperature and texture, then gently fold 600g ganache into 600g buttercream. Take care not to overwork, as the mixture can split easily.

TO ASSEMBLE THE CAKE
Trim the sponges (see page 150), then spread a thin covering of the chocolate buttercream onto the top of each layer.

Put some chocolate buttercream into a piping bag and pipe a small amount into each raspberry.

Arrange the raspberries over one of the cake layers and pipe some more buttercream in between the raspberries until you have a level surface. Place the next sponge layer on top.

Add another layer of raspberries and chocolate buttercream, as above, then position the final sponge layer on the top.

Place the cake on a turntable and mask the top and sides of the cake with the remaining chocolate buttercream, following the instructions on pages 152–53.

TO DECORATE
Decorate the top of the cake with a generous covering of fresh raspberries.

Store the cake in the fridge if not serving immediately, and serve at room temperature. Keep away from heat or direct sunlight. This cake will keep for about 3 days.

BLUEBERRY AND BUTTERMILK CAKE

I CALL THIS CAKE A CROWD PLEASER BECAUSE IT TASTES SO YUMMY, GOOEY AND CREAMY; IT ALMOST REMINDS ME OF A MILK SHAKE. YOU COULD EAT IT AT ANY TIME OF THE DAY, EVEN FOR BREAKFAST.

INGREDIENTS

For the buttermilk sponge
105g butter
275g caster sugar
½ teaspoon vanilla extract
2 eggs
250g plain flour, sifted
a pinch of salt
250g buttermilk
1 teaspoon bicarbonate of soda
1¼ teaspoons white wine vinegar
200g blueberries
2 tablespoons plain flour

For the vanilla syrup
150ml water
150g caster sugar
1 tablespoon vanilla extract

For the vanilla frosting
250g full-fat cream cheese, softened slightly
250g unsalted butter, softened
625g icing sugar, sifted
1 tablespoon vanilla extract
blueberry jam (for layering)

For the decoration
1 tablespoon blueberries
fresh mint leaves (optional)

EQUIPMENT

baking tool kit (see page 8)
layering tool kit (see page 8)
three 15cm sandwich tins
patterned side scraper
piping bag
round piping nozzle no. 3

Makes one 15cm cake, serving 8 generous slices.

METHOD

Make the sponge one day ahead.

TO MAKE THE BUTTERMILK SPONGE

Preheat the oven to 170°C/gas mark 3.

Line three 15cm sandwich tins with oil spray and greaseproof paper.

Place the butter, caster sugar and vanilla in an electric mixer and, using the paddle, beat at medium-high speed until the mixture is pale and fluffy.

Beat the eggs lightly in a separate bowl or jug, then slowly pour into the butter mixture with the paddle beating at medium speed. If it starts to curdle, add a tablespoon of flour to bring it back together.

Once the butter, sugar and eggs are combined, sift the 250g of flour and salt into a bowl and add a little to the mixture, followed by a little of the buttermilk, beating at low speed. Repeat until all the dry ingredients and buttermilk have been added and are just combined.

Stir the bicarbonate of soda into the vinegar and quickly add to the mixture.

Using a rubber spatula, fold through the batter to make sure everything is well combined.

Mix the blueberries with the remaining two tablespoons of flour, then gently fold into the cake batter.

Transfer the batter to the lined tins and carefully spread towards the edges with a step palette knife. The mixture should be high around the edges and dipped down in the centre, to ensure an even bake and level height.

Bake for 20–25 minutes. The sponge is cooked if it springs back when touched and the sides are coming away from the edges of the tin. Alternatively, insert a clean knife into the middle of the sponge; if it is cooked, the knife will come out clean.

While the sponges are baking, make a sugar syrup following the instructions on page 13 and flavour with vanilla extract.

Once the sponges are baked, remove from the oven and leave to rest for about 10 minutes. Brush the tops of the sponges with vanilla syrup (reserving some for the assembling stage and storing it in the fridge overnight).

Once just warm, run a knife all the way round the sides of the tins, remove the sponges and leave to cool completely on a wire rack.

Once cool, wrap the sponges in cling film and leave them to rest overnight at room temperature. This will ensure that all the moisture is sealed and the sponges firm up to the perfect texture for trimming and layering.

TO MAKE THE VANILLA FROSTING

Make a cream-cheese frosting following the instructions on page 12 and add the vanilla extract.

Chill for at least 2 hours, or until set.

TO ASSEMBLE THE CAKE

Trim the three sponge layers, soak the tops with more vanilla syrup and sandwich together using the blueberry jam for one layer and some of the vanilla frosting for the other. For instructions on how to trim and layer your cake, see pages 150–51.

Use vanilla frosting to mask the top and sides of the cake. See the guide to masking on pages 152–53. Chill for at least 1 hour (depending on the temperature of your fridge).

TO DECORATE

Mask the cake again, with a generous layer of vanilla frosting, and use a side scraper with a patterned edge to go around the side of the cake. Chill again until set.

Fill a small piping bag with the remaining vanilla frosting and pipe a loop pattern around the edge of the cake (see page 154).

Decorate the top of the cake with a small cluster of fresh blueberries and mint leaves.

If stored in the fridge, this cake will last for up to 5 days; however, it will taste at its best for the first 3 days. Serve at room temperature.

MILK AND HONEY CAKE

THIS CAKE WILL BRING BACK CHILDHOOD MEMORIES AND EVOKE FEELINGS OF COMFORT AND HAPPINESS. IT TASTES EXACTLY AS ITS NAME SUGGESTS AND IS THE PERFECT CAKE FOR KIDS – BUT GROWN-UPS WILL LIKE IT TOO.

INGREDIENTS

For the honeycomb
20g honey
25g glucose
100g caster sugar
40ml water
1 teaspoon bicarbonate of soda

For the buttermilk sponge
9 egg whites
250g caster sugar
50ml vanilla extract
335g plain flour
1 ½ tablespoons baking powder
a pinch of salt
4 egg yolks
175ml buttermilk
75g honeycomb (see above)

For the honey syrup
150ml water
150g caster sugar
2 tablespoons honey

For the honey frosting
250g full-fat cream cheese, softened slightly
250g unsalted butter, softened
625g icing sugar, sifted
4 tablespoons honey

For the decoration
A small amount of marzipan or sugar paste
Edible gold lustre (powder or spray)

EQUIPMENT

baking tool kit (see page 8)
layering tool kit (see page 8)
baking tray
sugar thermometer
three 15cm shallow round sandwich tins
bee silicon mould (see page 156)
soft artist brush

Makes one 15cm cake, serving 8 generous slices.

METHOD

Make the honeycomb a couple of hours before baking and store in an airtight container. Bake the sponge one day before assembling.

TO MAKE THE HONEYCOMB

Line a baking tray with greaseproof paper and cover with oil spray.

Place the honey, glucose, caster sugar and water in a large saucepan and bring to the boil.

Allow the mixture to reach 150°C, then carefully remove the saucepan from the heat.

Using a whisk, fold in the bicarbonate of soda, then gently pour onto the prepared baking tray. Do not spread out the mixture with a spatula or palette knife as it will knock out the air bubbles. Instead, pour it evenly over the tray.

Leave to harden for at least 30 minutes. Once cool, break two-thirds of the honeycomb into small pieces and cover the remainder with cling film to protect it from absorbing moisture from the air.

TO MAKE THE BUTTERMILK SPONGE

Preheat the oven to 170°C/gas mark 3.

Line three 15cm sandwich tins with oil spray and greaseproof paper.

Separate the eggs. Put the egg whites in an electric mixer and, using a whisk attachment, whip at high speed until they form soft peaks. Gradually add the sugar and vanillla extract, then beat until stiff and glossy.

Sift the flour, baking powder and salt into a bowl. Using a paddle attachment, mix the egg white mixture at low speed, incorporating the egg yolks one at a time. Keeping the mixer on a low setting, add a third of the sifted dry ingredients to the egg mixture, followed by a third of the buttermilk. Repeat until everything is well incorporated.

Fold in the honeycomb (there should be about a third left for decoration) and gently spoon the mixture into the prepared tins. Bake for 20–25 minutes or until the cakes spring back when gently prodded and a skewer comes out clean.

Once the sponges are baked, remove from the oven and leave to cool in the tins for about 10 minutes.

Run a knife all the way round the sides of the tins, remove the sponges and leave to cool completely on a wire cooling rack.

Wrap the sponges in cling film and leave to rest overnight at room temperature. This will ensure that all the moisture is sealed and that the sponges are the perfect texture for trimming and layering.

TO MAKE THE HONEY SYRUP

Make some sugar syrup, following the instructions on page 13. While still warm, add the honey and mix well.

TO MAKE THE HONEY FROSTING

Make some cream-cheese frosting, following the instructions on page 12.

Gently fold in the honey and allow to chill for at least 2 hours.

TO ASSEMBLE THE CAKE

Trim the three sponge layers and sandwich them together, adding honey frosting and honey syrup between the layers. For instructions, see pages 150–51.

Mask the top and sides of the cake with honey frosting. For masking tips, see pages 152–53.

TO DECORATE

Make a marzipan or sugar bee using the silicon mould.

Brush the bee with gold lustre and leave it to dry.

Brush or spray the remaining honeycomb pieces with gold lustre and then break into small pieces, sprinkle them on top of the cake. Do this at the last minute, as the honeycomb will start to melt once it's in touch with the frosting.

Press the bee onto the edge of the cake and serve.

This cake has a shelf life of up to 5 days if stored in the fridge; however, the honeycomb will start to melt after one day of exposure to air and humidity.

ROSE AND PISTACHIO CAKE

THIS IS A MOIST CAKE WITH A NUTTY TEXTURE AND A SUBTLE NOTE OF ROSE.
I DECORATED IT WITH A CONTEMPORARY STENCIL DESIGN, BUT YOU COULD
SCATTER OVER FRESH ROSE PETALS AND SERVE IT FOR A SPECIAL OCCASION
OR AS AN INDULGENT DESSERT.

INGREDIENTS

For the pistachio sponge

200g butter
200g caster sugar
2 tablespoons pistachio paste
4 eggs
100g pistachios, toasted and finely ground
200g self-raising flour
a pinch of salt

For the sugar syrup

150g water
150g caster sugar

For the rose buttercream

270g caster sugar
67ml water
330g butter
135g egg whites
2 tablespoons rose water, or to taste
pink food colour

For the sugar dust

5 tablespoons icing sugar
½ teaspoon edible green dust

EQUIPMENT

baking tool kit (see page 8)
layering tool kit (see page 8)
three 15cm round sandwich tins
floral scroll cake stencil (I used a stencil
from my own sugarcraft collection, but
others are available online)
small plastic sandwich bag

Makes one 15cm cake, serving 8 generous slices.

METHOD

Make the sponge one day ahead.

TO MAKE THE PISTACHIO SPONGE

Preheat the oven to 175°C/gas mark 4.

Line three 15cm sandwich tins with oil spray and greaseproof paper.

Place the butter, caster sugar and pistachio paste in an electric mixer and, using the paddle, beat at medium-high speed until pale and fluffy.

Lightly beat the eggs in a separate bowl or jug and, with the mixer on medium speed, slowly pour into the butter mixture. Add the ground pistachios and beat until combined.

Sift the flour and salt together and gently fold into the mixture.

Transfer the batter to the lined tins and gently spread out towards the edges with a step palette knife.

Bake for 20–25 minutes. The sponges are cooked when they spring back to the touch and the sides are coming away from the edges of the tin. To double-check, you could insert a clean knife into the middle of the sponge; if it is cooked, the knife will come out clean.

While the sponges are in the oven, make the sugar syrup following the instructions on page 13.

When they are baked, remove the sponges from the oven and leave to rest for about 10 minutes. Brush the tops of the sponges with syrup (reserving some for the assembling stage and storing it in the fridge overnight).

Run a knife all the way round the sides of the tins, remove the sponges and leave to cool completely on a wire rack.

Wrap the sponges in cling film and leave to rest overnight at room temperature. This will seal in all the moisture and ensure that the sponges are nice and firm, ready for trimming and layering.

TO MAKE THE ROSE MERINGUE BUTTERCREAM

Make some meringue buttercream following the instructions on page 10.

Add the rose water according to taste and a little pink food colour, and mix well. Be careful not to overwork the mixture as it can split.

TO MAKE THE SUGAR DUST

Put the icing sugar and edible green dust inside a small plastic bag and mix together until well combined.

TO ASSEMBLE THE CAKE

Trim the three sponges and soak with the sugar syrup. Sandwich together using the rose meringue buttercream. See pages 150–51 for instructions on how to trim and layer the cake.

Mask the top and sides of the cake using the remaining rose meringue buttercream (see pages 152–53). Chill the cake again.

TO DECORATE

When the final layer of buttercream is set and cold, position the floral stencil on the top of the cake so that it overhangs one side of the cake. (If the buttercream isn't quite set, the stencil could get stuck and leave a mark when you lift it off.) Sprinkle the sugar dust over the stencil, ensuring that all the cut-outs are well coated. Carefully lift the stencil and place it on the other side of the cake, then dust again.

Store the cake in the fridge if not serving immediately, and serve at room temperature. Keep away from heat or direct sunlight. The cake tastes best if consumed within 3 days of baking, but can last for up to 1 week if stored in the fridge.

SNOWBALL CAKE

THIS IS A VERY LIGHT, YET INDULGENT, CAKE WITH A CREAMY COCONUT TEXTURE AND A NUTTY TOASTED-ALMOND SPONGE.

INGREDIENTS

For the almond sponge
3 large eggs, separated
1 teaspoon vanilla extract
110g caster sugar
a pinch of salt
45g cornflour
½ teaspoon baking powder
90g ground almonds

For the vanilla syrup
150ml water
150g sugar
1 teaspoon vanilla extract (or to taste)

**For the coconut
meringue buttercream**
270g caster sugar
67ml water
135g egg whites
330g butter
15g organic creamed coconut

For the decoration
desiccated coconut

EQUIPMENT

baking tool kit (see page 8)
layering tool kit (see page 8)
three 15cm shallow round sandwich tins

Makes one 15cm cake, serving 8 generous slices.

METHOD

Make the sponge one day ahead.

TO MAKE THE ALMOND SPONGE

Preheat the oven to 175°C/gas mark 4.

Line three 15cm sandwich tins with oil spray and greaseproof paper.

In the bowl of an electric mixer, beat the egg yolks and vanilla. With the mixer on high speed, gradually add 60g of the caster sugar. Beat for about 5 minutes, until pale, thick and light. Transfer the egg-yolk mixture to a large bowl and set aside.

Place the egg whites and salt in a bowl and, using the electric mixer, beat on medium speed until soft peaks form. Increase the speed to high and gradually add the remaining sugar. Beat for about 4 minutes, until stiff and glossy.

Fold the egg-white mixture into the egg-yolk mixture.

Fold the remaining dry ingredients into the egg mixture, a third at a time.

Transfer the batter to the lined tins and gently spread it towards the edges using a step palette knife. The mixture should be higher around the edges of the tin than in the centre, to ensure an even bake and cake height.

Bake for 25–30 minutes. The sponge is cooked when it springs back to the touch and the sides are coming away from the edges of the tin. To be absolutely sure, insert a clean knife into the middle of the sponge; if it is cooked, the knife will come out clean.

While baking, make the sugar syrup following the instructions on page 13 and allow to cool. Add vanilla extract to taste.

Once the sponges are baked, remove from the oven and leave them to rest for about 10 minutes.

Brush the tops of the sponges with vanilla syrup.

Once just warm, run a knife all the way round the sides of the tins, transfer the sponges to a wire cooling rack and leave to cool completely.

Once cool, wrap the sponges in cling film and leave them to rest overnight at room temperature. This will ensure that all the moisture is sealed and the sponges are a good firm texture ready for trimming and layering.

TO MAKE THE COCONUT MERINGUE BUTTERCREAM

Make the meringue buttercream following the instructions on page 10.

Soften the creamed coconut following the instructions on the packet and gently fold into the meringue buttercream.

TO ASSEMBLE THE CAKE

Trim the three sponge layers and sandwich them together using the coconut meringue buttercream.

Mask the top and sides of the cake with the remaining buttercream.

For full instructions on how to trim, layer and mask your cake, turn to pages 150–53.

TO DECORATE

Place the dessicated coconut in a medium-sized bowl. Hold the chilled cake above the bowl at an angle and press the dessicated coconut around the sides. Catch the excess coconut in the bowl.

If stored in the fridge, this cake will last for up to 5 days; however, it will taste at its best if consumed within 3 days of baking. Serve at room temperature.

SALTED CARAMEL CAKE

THIS CAKE ROCKS! SORRY TO BE SO BLUNT, BUT IT REALLY DOES. IT IS SMOOTH, GOOEY, STICKY, SWEET AND SALTY, AND IS JAM-PACKED WITH LOTS OF CHOCOLATE AND CARAMEL. CAKE DOESN'T GET MUCH BETTER THAN THIS.

INGREDIENTS

For the caramel sponge
55g butter
125g caster sugar
75g dark brown sugar
2 teaspoons vanilla extract
2 eggs
140g plain flour
120g buttermilk
7.5g white wine vinegar
½ teaspoon bicarbonate of soda

For the chocolate sponge
100g butter
340g light brown sugar
100g plain chocolate drops (53% cocoa solids)
150ml milk
3 medium eggs
225g plain flour
2¼ tablespoons cocoa powder
¾ teaspoon bicarbonate of soda
¾ teaspoon baking powder
a pinch of salt

For the vanilla sponge
100g butter
100g caster sugar
½ teaspoon vanilla extract
2 medium eggs
100g self-raising flour, sifted
a pinch of salt

For the vanilla syrup
200ml water
200g sugar
1 tablespoon vanilla extract

For the salted caramel
450g sugar
150g water
45g glucose
300g whipping cream, slightly heated
120g butter
½ teaspoon salt

For the chocolate ganache
600g plain Belgian chocolate drops
450ml whipping cream
60g glucose

EQUIPMENT

baking tool kit (see page 8)
layering tool kit (see page 8)
20cm round sandwich tin
piping bag
cocktail stick

Makes one 20cm round cake, serving 12–16 generous slices.

METHOD

Make the sponges one day ahead.

TO MAKE THE CARAMEL SPONGE
Preheat the oven to 175°C/gas mark 4.

Line one 20cm sandwich tin with oil spray and greaseproof paper.

Place the butter, caster sugar, dark brown sugar and vanilla in an electric mixer and, using the paddle, beat at medium-high speed until pale and fluffy.

Lightly beat the eggs in a separate bowl or jug and, with the mixer on medium speed, slowly pour in the eggs. If the mixture starts to curdle, add a tablespoon of flour to bring it back together.

Once combined, mix in the flour and buttermilk, beating at low speed until just incorporated.

In a small bowl, combine the vinegar and bicarbonate of soda. Fold this quickly, but lightly, through the cake batter. Using a rubber spatula, fold through the batter to make sure everything is well combined.

Transfer the batter to the lined tin and gently spread it towards the edges with a step palette knife. Bake for 25–30 minutes.

The sponge is cooked when it springs back to the touch and the sides are coming away from the edges of the tin. If you insert a clean knife into the centre, it should come out clean. Remove from the oven and leave to rest for about 10 minutes.

While the sponge is baking, make the vanilla syrup following the instructions on page 13 and using the amounts given on page 34.

Once the sponge is baked, remove from the oven and leave to rest for about 10 minutes. Brush the top of the sponge with the vanilla syrup.

When just warm, run a knife all the way round the sides of the tin, transfer the sponge to a wire cooling rack and leave to cool completely.

Wrap the cooled sponge in cling film and leave it to rest overnight at room temperature. This will ensure

that all the moisture is sealed and the sponge is the perfect firm texture for trimming and layering.

TO MAKE THE CHOCOLATE SPONGE
Preheat the oven to 160°C/gas mark 3.

Line one 20cm sandwich tin with oil spray and greaseproof paper.

Put the butter and half of the brown sugar in an electric mixer and, using the paddle, beat at medium-high speed until pale and fluffy.

Meanwhile, place the chocolate drops, milk and remaining sugar in a deep saucepan and bring to the boil, stirring occasionally.

Slowly add the eggs to the mixer. Sift together the flour, cocoa powder, bicarbonate of soda, baking powder and salt and add to the mixture while beating on slow speed.

Pour the hot chocolate mixture into a jug and slowly add it to the batter while mixing on slow speed. Take care, as the hot mixture could splash you. Once combined, pour the hot batter into the prepared tin.

Bake for 20–30 minutes. If you insert a clean knife into the middle of the sponge to check that it is cooked, the knife will come out almost clean – this chocolate cake should be slightly gooey in texture.

Once cooked, let the cake rest in the tin for about 10 minutes, then transfer to a wire rack to cool.

Once completely cool, wrap the sponge in cling film and leave to rest overnight at room temperature.

TO MAKE THE VANILLA SPONGE
Preheat the oven to 175°C/gas mark 4.

Line one 20cm sandwich tin with oil spray and greaseproof paper.

Place the butter, caster sugar and vanilla in an electric mixer and, using the paddle, beat at medium-high speed until pale and fluffy.

Lightly beat the eggs in a separate bowl or jug and

slowly pour into the mixture with the mixer on medium speed. If the mixture starts to curdle, add a tablespoon of flour to bring it back together.

Once the mixture is well incorporated, mix in the flour and salt at low speed until just combined. Using a rubber spatula, fold through the batter to make sure everything is well combined.

Transfer the batter to the lined tin and spread towards the edges with a step palette knife. The mixture should be high around the edges and dip down in the middle, to ensure an even bake and level height.

Bake for 20–25 minutes. Check that the sponge is cooked (as with the caramel sponge, a knife pushed into the centre should come out clean).

Once the sponge is baked, remove from the oven and leave to rest for about 10 minutes. Brush the top of the sponge with the vanilla syrup.

When the sponge is just warm, run a knife all the way round the sides of the tin, transfer to a wire cooling rack and leave to cool completely.

Wrap the cooled sponge in cling film and leave to rest overnight at room temperature.

TO MAKE THE SALTED CARAMEL
Heat the sugar, water and glucose in a medium saucepan over a moderate heat, stirring continuously with a rubber spatula. The sugar will melt into a thick amber liquid as you stir. Do not let the sugar burn.

Once the sugar has caramelised, slowly add the cream. Be careful here, as the caramel will bubble rapidly when the cream is added.

Add the butter to the caramel, stirring until melted. This will take 2–3 minutes. Let the mixture boil for 1 minute – it will rise in the pan as it boils.

Remove the caramel from the heat and stir in ½ teaspoon of salt. Cover well and cool before using.

TO MAKE THE CHOCOLATE GANACHE
Make the ganache following the instructions on page 13, using the amounts given on page 34, and allow to cool to room temperature.

TO ASSEMBLE THE CAKE
Trim the three sponge layers.

Fill a piping bag with chocolate ganache, take the chocolate and caramel sponges and pipe a ring of ganache around the edge of each one.

Using a palette knife, fill each ring with salted caramel, then sandwich the layers together with the chocolate at the bottom, caramel in the middle and vanilla on the top. See pages 150–51 for full instructions on how to trim and layer your cakes.

Place the cake on a turntable and mask with chocolate ganache (see pages 152–53). Chill for at least 2 hours.

TO DECORATE
Place a wire rack over a large plate or tray. Pour the remaining ganache into a microwavable jug. Heat the ganache in the microwave until smooth and pourable.

Place the cake on the wire rack and pour the ganache over the cake, ensuring that the sides are well covered (see steps 1–3).

Use a large palette knife to smooth the top and remove any excess ganache (see step 4).

Put the remaining salted caramel into a piping bag and pipe a spiral pattern on top of the cake. If the caramel is too stiff, soften it in the microwave (see steps 5–7).

Using a toothpick, make lines from the centre of the spiral to the edges of the cake to create a spider-web pattern (see steps 8–9).

Using a large palette knife, carefully lift the cake from the rack and place it on your cake stand.

To maintain the sheen on the ganache, let the glaze set at room temperature.

The ganache that dripped onto the plate can be reused. Any remaining ganache can be kept for up to 2 weeks in an airtight container in the fridge.

Store the cake in the fridge if not serving on the same day. Always serve at room temperature. The cake tastes best within the first 3 days of baking, but will last for up to one week if stored in the fridge.

SALTED CARAMEL CAKE

VANILLA CLOUD CAKE

AS THE NAME SUGGESTS, THIS CAKE HAS A HEAVENLY LIGHT TEXTURE AND TASTES SMOOTH AND SQUISHY. IT IS THE PERFECT CAKE FOR KIDS' BIRTHDAYS AND BABY CELEBRATIONS.

INGREDIENTS

For the chiffon sponge
80g egg yolks
1 tablespoon vanilla extract
225g caster sugar
75ml vegetable oil
165g egg whites
a pinch of cream of tartar
a pinch of salt
225g plain flour
15g baking powder
120ml milk

**For the vanilla
meringue buttercream**
270g caster sugar
67ml water
135g egg whites
330g butter
1 tablespoon vanilla extract
a little pink food paste colour

For the vanilla syrup
150ml water
150g caster sugar
1 tablespoon vanilla extract

For the decoration
icing sugar, for dusting

EQUIPMENT

baking tool kit (see page 8)
layering tool kit (see page 8)
three 15cm round sandwich tins
Bows & Swags bow or cloud stencil
(both available from Peggy's sugarcraft collection)

Makes one 15cm pink cake, serving 8 generous slices.
Multiply the amounts by 3 for a 25cm cake.

METHOD

Make the sponge one day ahead.

TO MAKE THE CHIFFON SPONGE
Preheat the oven to 175°C/gas mark 4.

Line three 15cm sandwich tins with oil spray and greaseproof paper.

Place the egg yolks, vanilla extract. and a little of the sugar in an electric mixer and using the whisk attachment, beat until pale and fluffy. Add the oil slowly and continue to beat until thick and pale.

Beat the egg whites, cream of tartar and salt in the mixer and, using the whisk attachment, beat at medium-high speed until the mixture forms soft peaks.

With the mixer still running, slowly pour in the remaining sugar and beat until the mixture is glossy and holds stiff peaks.

Sift the flour and baking powder into a medium-sized bowl and add to the egg-yolk mixture a little at a time, gently folding after each addition to incorporate. Add the milk and fold in the stiff egg whites.

Transfer the batter to the lined tins and gently spread it towards the edges with a step palette knife. The mixture should be higher around the edges of each tin and dipping in the centre; this will ensure that the sponges bake evenly and are level.

Bake for 20–25 minutes. Insert a clean knife into the middle of each sponge; if they are cooked, the knife will come out clean.

While baking, make the sugar syrup following the instructions on page 13. Add the vanilla extract and mix well.

Once the sponges are baked, remove from the oven and leave to rest for about 10 minutes. Brush the tops of the sponges with vanilla syrup (reserving some for the assembling stage and storing it in the fridge overnight).

Once just warm, run a knife all the way round the sides of the tins, remove the sponges and leave to cool completely on a wire rack.

Once cool, wrap the sponges in cling film and leave to rest overnight at room temperature. This will ensure that all the moisture is sealed and that the sponges are a good firm texture for trimming and layering.

TO MAKE THE VANILLA MERINGUE BUTTERCREAM
Follow the instructions for meringue buttercream on page 10.

Mix a small amount of the buttercream with the vanilla extract and a little pink food colour until all the colour has dissolved.

Slowly add the mixture to the remaining buttercream and fold through gently, taking care not to overwork.

TO ASSEMBLE THE CAKE
Trim the three sponge layers, soak with more of the vanilla syrup and sandwich together using the pink vanilla meringue buttercream. For full instructions, see pages 150–51.

Place the cake on a turntable and mask the top and sides with the remaining meringue buttercream. For a detailed guide to masking, turn to pages 152–53.

TO DECORATE
Centre the cake stencil on the top of the cold masked cake and dust the surface liberally with icing sugar.

Carefully lift the stencil off the cake to reveal the ribbon pattern.

Store the cake in the fridge if not serving immediately, and serve at room temperature. Keep away from heat or direct sunlight. The cake tastes best if consumed within 3 days of baking, but can last for up to a week if stored in the fridge.

TO MAKE THE LIGHT BLUE CLOUD CAKE
Triple the sponge recipe and bake in three 25cm sandwich tins.

Slice each layer in half and sandwich with light blue vanilla meringue buttercream.

Mask with light blue vanilla meringue buttercream, and use a cloud stencil to decorate.

COOKIES AND CREAM CAKE

FOLLOWING THE SUCCESS OF MY CUPCAKE VERSION OF THIS CAKE – WHICH WAS
DESCRIBED BY ONE OF MY CUSTOMERS AS 'LIFE CHANGING' – I FELT COMPELLED TO
TURN IT INTO A LAYER CAKE. SEE WHAT YOU THINK …

INGREDIENTS

For the cookies & cream sponge
300g butter
300g caster sugar
1 tablespoon vanilla extract
6 eggs
300g self-raising flour
¾ teaspoon baking powder
a pinch of salt
150g Oreo cookies, crushed

For the vanilla syrup
150ml water
150g sugar
1 teaspoon vanilla extract

For the cookie frosting
250g cream cheese, softened
250g unsalted butter, softened
625g icing sugar, sifted
1 tablespoon vanilla extract
200g Oreo cookies, finely crushed

For the decoration
16 mini Oreo cookies

EQUIPMENT

baking tool kit (see page 8)
layering tool kit (see page 8)
four 15cm round sandwich tins
piping bag
medium round piping nozzle

Makes one 15cm round cake, serving 8 generous slices.

METHOD

Make the sponge one day ahead.

TO MAKE THE COOKIE AND CREAM SPONGE
Preheat the oven to 170°C/gas mark 3.

Line four 15cm sandwich tins with oil spray and greaseproof paper.

Place the butter, sugar and vanilla extract in an electric mixer and, using the paddle, beat at medium-high speed until pale and fluffy.

Lightly beat the eggs in a separate bowl or jug and, with the mixer set at medium speed, slowly pour into the butter mixture. If it starts to curdle, add a tablespoon of flour to bring it back together.

Sift in the flour, baking powder and salt and fold until the batter is just combined.

Add the crushed cookies.

Bake for 20–25 minutes. The sponges are cooked when they spring back to the touch and the sides are coming away from the edges of the tins. To double-check, you could insert a clean knife into the middle of the sponges; if they are cooked, the knife will come out clean.

While the sponges are in the oven, make the vanilla sugar syrup following the instructions on page 13. Add the vanilla extract to taste.

Once the sponges are baked, remove from the oven and leave them to rest for about 10 minutes.

Brush the tops of the sponges with vanilla syrup (reserving some for the assembling stage and storing it in the fridge overnight).

Once just warm, run a knife all the way round the sides of the tins, remove the sponges and leave to cool completely on a wire cooling rack.

Wrap the cooled sponges in cling film and leave them to rest overnight at room temperature. This will ensure that all the moisture is sealed and the sponges are the perfect firm texture for trimming and layering.

TO MAKE THE COOKIE FROSTING
Make a cream-cheese frosting following the instructions on page 12.

Gently fold in the vanilla and crushed Oreo cookies and chill for at least 2 hours or until set.

TO ASSEMBLE THE CAKE
Trim the four sponge layers, soak with more vanilla syrup and sandwich together using the cookie frosting. See pages 150–51 for further instructions on how to trim and layer the sponges.

Mask the top and sides of the cake with the remaining cookies and frosting. See pages 152–53 for a step-by-step guide to masking.

TO DECORATE
Place the remaining cookie frosting in a piping bag fitted with a medium round nozzle.

Pipe 16 evenly-spaced small dots around the edge of the cake and top each one with a mini Oreo cookie.

If stored in the fridge, this cake will last for up to 5 days; however, it tastes best if consumed within the first 3 days of baking. Serve at room temperature.

LEMON, RASPBERRY AND ROSE CAKE

THIS IS A LOVELY FLAVOUR COMBINATION THAT WORKS REALLY WELL FOR A SUMMER OCCASION SUCH AS A GARDEN TEA PARTY. FOR A CONTEMPORARY LOOK, I HAVE COLOUR-BLOCKED THE TOP OF THE CAKE WITH A LAYER OF ROSE PETAL FRAGMENTS. IF YOU PREFER A MORE TRADITIONAL DESIGN, YOU COULD RE-CREATE THE CAKE SHOWN ON THE COVER INSTEAD.

INGREDIENTS

For the lemon sponge
200g salted butter
200g caster sugar
zest of 2 unwaxed lemons
4 medium eggs, at room temperature
200g self-raising flour, sifted

For the lemon syrup
150ml lemon juice
150g caster sugar

For the raspberry meringue buttercream
270g caster sugar
67ml water
135g egg whites
330g butter
160g raspberry purée
raspberry extract (to taste)

For the decoration
about 3 tablespoons rose petal fragments, glazed
icing sugar and fresh raspberries (for cover design only)

EQUIPMENT

baking tool kit (see page 8)
layering tool kit (see page 8)
three 15cm round sandwich tins
For cover design only:
Peggy's cake stencil (included with this book)
piping bag
medium star piping nozzle

Makes one 15cm cake, serving 8 generous slices.

METHOD

Make the sponge one day ahead.

TO MAKE THE LEMON SPONGE

Preheat the oven to 175°C/gas mark 4.

Line three 15cm sandwich tins with oil spray and greaseproof paper.

Place the butter, caster sugar and lemon zest in an electric mixer and, using the paddle, beat at medium-high speed until pale and fluffy.

Lightly beat the eggs in a separate bowl or jug and, with the mixer set at medium speed, slowly pour into the mixture. If it starts to curdle, add a tablespoon of flour to bring it back together.

Once the butter, sugar and eggs are combined, add the flour with the mixer set at low speed, until just incorporated.

Using the rubber spatula, fold through the batter to make sure everything is well combined.

Transfer the batter to the lined tins and gently spread towards the edges with a step palette knife. The mixture should be higher around the edges of the tins than in the centre, to ensure an even bake and level cake height.

Bake for 20–25 minutes. The sponges are cooked when they spring back to the touch and the sides are coming away from the edges of the tin. You could also insert a clean knife into the middle of each sponge; if they are cooked, the knife will come out clean.

While the sponges are in the oven, make a lemon sugar syrup following the instructions on page 13, but replacing the water with lemon juice.

Once the sponges are baked, remove from the oven and allow them to rest for about 10 minutes. Brush the tops of the sponges with lemon syrup (reserving some for the assembling stage and storing it in the fridge overnight).

Once just warm, run a knife all the way round the sides of the tins, remove the sponges and leave to cool completely on a wire rack.

Wrap the cooled sponges in cling film and leave to rest overnight at room temperature. This will ensure that all the moisture is sealed and the sponges firm up to the ideal texture for trimming and layering.

TO MAKE THE RASPBERRY MERINGUE BUTTERCREAM

Put the raspberry purée in a small saucepan, bring to the boil and simmer until reduced to half. Chill until cool.

Make the meringue buttercream following the instructions on page 10.

Add a little meringue buttercream to the raspberry purée and mix until well combined.

Gently fold into the remaining meringue buttercream and add the raspberry extract to taste. If the mixture splits, whip it with an electric mixer until smooth.

TO ASSEMBLE THE CAKE

Trim the three sponge layers, soak with more lemon syrup and sandwich together using some of the raspberry meringue buttercream. If you wish to recreate the cake shown on the front of the book, sprinkle the rose petal fragments between the layers. For full instructions on how to trim and layer your cake, turn to pages 150–51.

Use meringue buttercream to mask the top and sides of the cake (see pages 152–53).

TO DECORATE

Generously sprinkle the rose petal fragments over the top of the cake.

If you are recreating the design shown on the cover, decorate the top of the cake using the stencil and a good dusting of icing sugar, then pipe small rosettes of raspberry meringue buttercream around the edge and finish with fresh raspberries.

FRENCH VIOLET CAKE
(GÂTEAU AUX FLEUR DE VIOLETTES)

THIS RECIPE PAYS TRIBUTE TO A BEAUTIFUL FRENCH ARTISAN VILLAGE CALLED 'TOURRETTES-SUR-LOUP', WHERE I STAYED LAST SUMMER. IT IS RENOWNED FOR ITS CULTURE OF VIOLETS AND CONFECTIONS, WHICH INSPIRED ME TO CREATE THIS DELECTABLE ELEGANT CAKE.

INGREDIENTS

For the chiffon sponge

80g egg yolks
225g caster sugar
75ml vegetable oil
165g egg whites
a pinch of cream of tartar
a pinch of salt
2 teaspoons vanilla extract
225g plain flour
15g baking powder
120g milk

For the vanilla syrup

150ml water
150ml caster sugar
1 tablespoon vanilla extract

For the violet meringue buttercream

270g caster sugar
67ml water
135g egg whites
330g butter
1 handful of violet petal fragments
a few drops of violet extract (to taste)
a little violet food paste colour

For the decoration

icing sugar
1 tablespoon crystallised whole violets

EQUIPMENT

baking tool kit (see page 8)
layering tool kit (see page 8)
three 15cm round sandwich tins
Peggy's cake stencil (included with this book)
piping bag
medium star piping nozzle

Makes one 15cm cake, serving 8 generous slices.

METHOD

Make the sponge one day ahead.

TO MAKE THE CHIFFON SPONGE

Preheat the oven to 175°C/gas mark 4.

Line three 15cm sandwich tins with oil spray and greaseproof paper.

Place the egg yolks in an electric mixer with a little of the sugar and, using the whisk attachment, beat at medium-high speed until pale and fluffy. Add the oil slowly and beat until thick and pale.

Put the egg whites, cream of tartar and salt in the electric mixer and, again using the whisk attachment, beat at medium-high speed until the mixture forms soft peaks.

With the mixer still running, slowly pour in the remaining sugar and beat until the mixture is glossy and holds stiff peaks. Beat in the vanilla extract.

Sift the flour and baking powder into a medium bowl and gradually add to the egg-yolk mixture, gently folding after each addition to incorporate. Add the milk and fold in the stiff egg whites.

Transfer the batter to the lined tins and gently spread it towards the edges with a step palette knife.

Bake for 20–25 minutes. The sponge is cooked when it springs back to the touch and the sides are coming away from the edges of the tin. To double-check, you could insert a clean knife into the middle of the sponge; if it is cooked, the knife will come out clean.

While the sponges are in the oven, make the sugar syrup following the instructions on page 13, then add the vanilla extract and mix well.

Once the sponges are baked, remove from the oven and allow them to rest for about 10 minutes. Brush the tops of the sponges with vanilla syrup (reserving some for the assembling stage and storing it in the fridge overnight).

Run a knife all the way round the sides of the tins and transfer the sponges to a wire cooling rack and leave to cool completely.

Once cool, wrap the sponges in cling film and leave to rest overnight at room temperature. This will ensure that all the moisture is sealed and the sponges are a nice firm texture, ready for trimming and layering.

TO MAKE THE VIOLET MERINGUE BUTTERCREAM

Make some meringue buttercream following the instructions on page 10.

Take 200g of the meringue buttercream and fold through the violet petal fragments and violet extract (add to taste). This will be used for the filling.

To the remaining buttercream add a little violet food paste colour and violet extract (add to taste). This will be used for masking.

TO ASSEMBLE THE CAKE

Trim the three sponge layers, soak the tops with vanilla syrup and sandwich together using the violet meringue buttercream with the petal fragments added. Turn to pages 150–51 for instructions on how to trim and layer your cake.

Place the cake on a turntable and mask with the violet-coloured meringue buttercream. See pages 152–53 for advice on how to mask the cake.

Chill the cake for at least 1 hour, or until the buttercream is set, before applying the final coat.

TO DECORATE THE CAKE

Centre the stencil on top of the chilled cake (see step 1, overleaf) and dust liberally with icing sugar, ensuring that all the cut-outs are well coated (see step 2). Carefully lift the stencil off the cake.

Attach the star nozzle to the piping bag and fill with the remaining violet-coloured meringue buttercream. Pipe rosettes around the edge of the cake, spacing them evenly over the pattern (see steps 3–4).

Top each rosette with a crystallised violet.

Refrigerate if not serving immediately, and serve at room temperature. Keep away from heat and direct sunlight. This cake is best eaten within 3 days, but will last for up to 1 week if stored in the fridge.

RED VELVET CAKE

THIS IS AN ALL-TIME CLASSIC AND A FIRM FAVOURITE AT MY CAKE SHOP – PERFECT
IF YOU WANT TO BAKE YOUR WAY INTO SOMEONE'S HEART.

INGREDIENTS

For the red velvet sponge
105g butter
275g caster sugar
1 teaspoon vanilla extract
about ½ teaspoon extra-red food colour
250g buttermilk
2 medium-sized eggs
235g plain flour
15g cocoa powder
2 pinches of salt
1 teaspoon bicarbonate of soda
1 ¼ teaspoons white wine vinegar

For the vanilla frosting
250g full-fat cream cheese, softened slightly
250g unsalted butter, softened
625g icing sugar, sifted
1 tablespoon vanilla extract

For the decoration
red velvet cake crumbs

EQUIPMENT

baking tool kit (see page 8)
layering tool kit (see page 8)
three 15cm shallow round sandwich tins
heart cake stencil (you can easily make your
own using a sheet of card or paper and a pair
of scissors)

Makes one 15cm cake, serving 8 generous slices.

METHOD

Make the sponge one day ahead.

TO MAKE THE RED VELVET SPONGE
Preheat the oven to 170°C/gas mark 3.

Line three 15cm sandwich tins with oil spray and greaseproof paper.

Place the butter, caster sugar and vanilla in an electric mixer and, using the paddle, beat at medium-high speed until pale and fluffy.

Mix the red food colour with the buttermilk, making sure there are no lumps.

Lightly beat the eggs in a separate bowl or jug and, with the mixer set at medium speed, slowly pour into the butter mixture. If the mixture starts to curdle, add a tablespoon of flour to bring it back together.

Sift the flour, cocoa powder and salt together and, once the butter, sugar and eggs are combined, add to the mixer with the coloured buttermilk and beat at low speed until just incorporated.

Whisk together the bicarbonate of soda and vinegar and quickly add to the cake batter.

Using the rubber spatula, fold through the batter to make sure everything is well combined.

Transfer the batter to the lined tins and gently spread it towards the edges with a step palette knife.

Bake for 20–25 minutes. The sponge is cooked when it springs back to the touch and the sides are coming away from the edges of the tin. You could also insert a clean knife into the middle of the sponge; if it is cooked, the knife will come out clean.

Once the sponges are baked, remove from the oven and leave to rest for about 10 minutes.

When the sponges are just warm, run a knife all the way round the sides of the tins, transfer to a wire cooling rack and leave to cool completely.

Once cool, wrap the sponges in cling film and leave them to rest overnight at room temperature.

This will ensure that all the moisture is sealed and the sponges firm up to the ideal texture for trimming and layering.

TO MAKE THE VANILLA FROSTING
Make a cream-cheese frosting following the instructions on page 12, then flavour with the vanilla extract.

Chill for at least 2 hours, or until set.

TO ASSEMBLE THE CAKE
Trim the sponges (reserving the trimmings for decoration) and sandwich the layers together using the vanilla frosting. See pages 150–51 for trimming and layering tips.

Mask the top and sides of the cake using the remaining vanilla frosting. See pages 152–53 for instructions on how to mask the cake.

TO DECORATE
Preheat the oven to 100°C/gas mark ¼.

Take all the trimmings from the sponges and place them on a lined baking tray.

Put them in the oven to dry out, until hard.

Put the cake trimmings in a food processor and whizz until you have a fine crumb.

Centre the heart cake stencil on the top of the cake, and dust the surface liberally with the red velvet cake crumbs.

Carefully lift the stencil off the cake to reveal the heart pattern.

Store the cake in the fridge if not serving immediately. The cake has a shelf life of up to 5 days but tastes best if consumed within 3 days.

Serve at room temperature.

TOFFEE APPLE CAKE

THIS IS A DELICIOUSLY MOIST APPLE CAKE, PACKED WITH NUTS AND SPICES.
I DECORATED IT WITH TINY APPLES FROM MY NEIGHBOUR'S GARDEN,
DIPPED IN GOLDEN CARAMEL.

INGREDIENTS

For the spiced apple sponge
225g unsalted butter
225g light brown sugar
1 tablespoon vanilla extract
4 medium eggs
240g self-raising flour
1 tablespoon ground cinnamon
a pinch of salt
200g Bramley apples, peeled and chopped
50g hazelnuts, toasted and finely chopped
zest of 1 unwaxed lemon

For the vanilla syrup
150ml water
150g caster sugar
1 tablespoon vanilla extract (or to taste)

For the caramel frosting
250g cream cheese, softened
250g unsalted butter, softened
625g icing sugar, sifted
150g dulce de leche (alternatively, use caramel
made from sweetened condensed milk)

For the dipping caramel
225g brown sugar
110ml water
½ teaspoon vinegar
30ml golden syrup
25g butter

For the decoration
3 mini crab apples
bay leaves or apple leaves

EQUIPMENT

baking tool kit (see page 8)
layering tool kit (see page 8)
three 15cm round sandwich tins
sugar thermometer
piping bag
large round piping nozzle

Makes one 15cm round cake, serving 8 generous slices.

LOVE LAYER CAKES

METHOD

Make the sponge one day ahead.

TO MAKE THE SPICED APPLE SPONGE

Preheat the oven to 175°C/gas mark 4.

Line three 15cm sandwich tins with oil spray and greaseproof paper.

Place the butter, sugar and vanilla extract in an electric mixer and, using the paddle, beat at medium-high speed until pale and fluffy.

Lightly beat the eggs in a separate bowl or jug and slowly pour into the mixer, while beating at medium speed. If the mixture starts to curdle, add a tablespoon of flour to bring it back together.

Sift the flour, cinnamon and salt into a bowl and fold into the batter until just combined.

Fold in the apple, hazelnuts and lemon zest, transfer the batter to the lined tins and gently spread it out towards the edges with a step palette knife. The mixture should be higher around the edges than in the middle, to ensure that the cake bakes evenly and that the height is level.

Bake for 20–25 minutes. The sponges are cooked when they spring back to the touch and the sides are starting to come away from the edges of the tins. To double-check, you could insert a clean knife into the middle of the sponge; if it is cooked, the knife will come out clean.

While the sponges are in the oven, make the sugar syrup following the instructions on page 13, then add the vanilla extract to taste.

When the sponges are baked, remove from the oven and leave them to rest for about 10 minutes. Brush the tops of the sponges with vanilla syrup (reserving some for the assembling stage and storing it in the fridge overnight).

Once just warm, run a knife all the way round the sides of the tins, remove the sponges and leave to cool completely on a wire rack.

When the sponges are cool, wrap them in cling film and leave them to rest overnight at room temperature. This will ensure that all the moisture is sealed and that the sponges are a good firm texture for trimming and layering.

TO MAKE THE CARAMEL FROSTING

Make a cream-cheese frosting following the instructions on page 12, then gently fold in the dulce de leche.

TO MAKE THE DIPPING CARAMEL

Put the sugar and water in a saucepan and place over a moderate heat, stirring lightly with a rubber spatula, until the sugar has dissolved.

Stir in the vinegar, syrup and butter, then bring to the boil, stirring continuously until the caramel reaches 138°C.

Immediately dip the apples in the caramel and leave to harden on a lightly oiled tray or greaseproof paper. (See steps 1–4, opposite.)

Dip the tips of the bay leaf stalks in the caramel and stick them to the tops of the apples.

TO ASSEMBLE THE CAKE

Trim the three sponge layers and soak the tops with vanilla syrup, as shown on pages 150–51.

Put the frosting in a piping bag fitted with a large round nozzle. Pipe a ring of large dots around the outside of the bottom layer, then pipe a swirl in the centre and place the second sponge layer on top. Repeat the piping on the next layer, then put the last sponge in place. (See steps 5–6.)

TO DECORATE

Repeat the piped pattern on the top of the cake and, using a palette knife, drag each dot towards the middle. (See steps 7–9.)

Place 3 mini toffee apples in the centre.

This cake has a shelf life of up to 3 days if stored in the fridge. Serve at room temperature.

BLACK AND WHITE DEVIL'S FOOD CAKE

THIS CHOCOLATE AND VANILLA CAKE IS TRULY DELICIOUS AND THE MONOCHROME LAYERS LOOK STRIKING WHEN CUT INTO SLICES.

INGREDIENTS

For the devil's food sponge
150g cocoa powder, sifted
300g dark brown muscovado sugar
750ml boiling water
375g unsalted butter
450g light brown sugar
2 tablespoons vanilla extract
6 large eggs
675g plain flour, sifted
1½ teaspoons baking powder, sifted
1½ teaspoons bicarbonate of soda, sifted
a pinch of salt
a little black food colour

For the sugar syrup
200ml water
200g sugar

For the vanilla frosting
375g cream cheese, softened
375g unsalted butter, softened
950g icing sugar, sifted
1 tablespoon vanilla extract

For the decoration
devil's food cake crumbs

EQUIPMENT

baking tool kit (see page 8)
layering tool kit (see page 8)
five 20cm round sandwich tins
patterned side scraper

Makes one 15cm round cake, serving 8–12 slices.

METHOD

Make the sponge one day ahead.

TO MAKE THE DEVIL'S FOOD SPONGE
Preheat the oven to 175°C/gas mark 4.

Line five 20cm sandwich tins with oil spray and greaseproof paper. (The sponges can be sliced in half if you don't have enough tins.)

Put the cocoa and dark muscovado sugar in a bowl and pour over the boiling water. Whisk to combine, then set aside.

In an electric mixer, cream together the butter, light brown sugar and vanilla extract, beating well until pale and fluffy.

Lightly beat the eggs in a separate bowl or jug and slowly pour into the mixer, set at medium speed.

Combine the dry ingredients, then gradually add to the mixer, alternating with the cocoa mixture. Scrape the sides of the bowl with a spatula, to ensure that everything is incorporated.

Fold in the black food colour until the batter takes on a muddy brown colour, then transfer to the lined tins.

Bake for 20–25 minutes. The sponge is cooked when it springs back to the touch and the sides are coming away from the edges of the tin. You could also insert a clean knife into the middle of the sponge; if it is cooked, the knife will come out clean.

While baking, make the sugar syrup following the instructions on page 13 but using the amounts given on page 68.

Once the sponges are baked, remove from the oven and allow them to rest for about 10 minutes.

Brush the tops of the sponges with sugar syrup (reserving some for the assembling stage and storing it in the fridge overnight).

Once just warm, run a knife all the way round the sides of the tins, remove the sponges and leave to cool completely on a wire cooling rack.

Wrapped the cooled sponges in cling film and leave them to rest overnight at room temperature. This will ensure that all the moisture is sealed and that the sponges are the perfect firm texture for trimming and layering.

TO MAKE THE VANILLA FROSTING
Make a cream-cheese frosting following the instructions on page 12, using the amounts given on page 68.

Gently fold in the vanilla extract and chill for at least 2 hours, or until set.

TO ASSEMBLE THE CAKE
Trim the five sponge layers, soak the tops with sugar syrup and sandwich together using the vanilla frosting. Reserve the trimmings for the decoration. See pages 150–51 for trimming and layering instructions.

Mask the top and sides of the cake with the remaining vanilla cream-cheese frosting (see pages 152–53).

To apply the final coat of masking, use a side scraper with a patterned edge.

TO DECORATE
Preheat the oven to 100°C/gas mark ¼.

Place all the cake trimmings on a lined baking tray and put them in the oven to dry out.

Once dry and hard, put the trimmings into a food processor and whizz until you have a fine dust.

Sprinkle the chocolate dust evenly over the top of the cake.

PASSION FRUIT AND MASCARPONE CAKE

A REFRESHING TROPICAL CAKE FOR HOT SUMMER DAYS.

INGREDIENTS

For the vanilla sponge

200g butter

200g caster sugar

1 tablespoon vanilla extract

4 eggs

200g self-raising flour, sifted

For the vanilla syrup

150ml water

150g sugar

1 teaspoon vanilla extract (or to taste)

For the mango frosting

200g unsalted butter, softened

500g icing sugar

300g mascarpone, softened slightly

30g mango purée

For the passion fruit jelly

3 large gelatine leaves

200g passion fruit purée

50ml water

50g sugar

2 passion fruit

To decorate

200g coconut shavings

EQUIPMENT

baking tool kit (see page 8)

layering tool kit (see page 8)

three 15cm round sandwich tins

baking tray

blowtorch (if needed)

Makes one 15cm cake, serving 8 generous slices.

METHOD

Make the sponge one day ahead.

TO MAKE THE VANILLA SPONGE
Preheat the oven to 175°C/gas mark 4.

Line three 15cm sandwich tins with oil spray and greaseproof paper.

Place the butter, caster sugar and vanilla in an electric mixer and, using the paddle, beat at medium-high speed until pale and fluffy.

Lightly beat the eggs in a separate bowl or jug and slowly pour into the mixer, beating at medium speed. If the mixture starts to curdle, add a little flour.

Once the butter, sugar and eggs are combined, mix the flour at low speed until it is just incorporated.

Using a rubber spatula, fold through the batter to make sure everything is well combined.

Bake for 20–25 minutes. When the sponge springs back to the touch and the sides are coming away from the edges of the tin, it is cooked. You could also insert a clean knife into the centre of the sponge; if it is cooked, the knife will come out clean.

While the sponges are baking, make the vanilla sugar syrup by following the instructions on page 13, then adding vanilla extract to taste.

Once the sponges are baked, remove from the oven and leave them to rest for about 10 minutes. Using a pastry brush, soak the tops of the sponges with some of the vanilla syrup.

When just warm, run a knife all the way round the sides of the tins, transfer the sponges to a wire rack and leave to cool completely.

Wrap the cooled sponges in cling film and leave to rest overnight at room temperature. This will seal in all the moisture and firm up the sponges so they are the perfect texture for trimming and layering.

TO MAKE THE MANGO FROSTING
Make some mascarpone frosting following the instructions on page 12.

Gently fold in the mango purée. Chill for about 2 hours, or until set.

TO MAKE THE PASSION FRUIT JELLY
Soak the leaf gelatine in cold water for about 3 minutes.

Put the passion fruit purée, water and sugar in a small saucepan and bring to the boil.

Remove from the heat and add the drained leaf gelatine. Stir well and pass through a sieve.

Add the pulp of the fresh passion fruit.

Line two 15cm round cake tins with cling film. Divide the jelly mixture between the two tins and refrigerate for 30 minutes–1 hour, or until set.

TO TOAST THE COCONUT SHAVINGS
Preheat the oven to 175°C/gas mark 4.

Spread out the coconut shavings on a baking tray and put in the oven for about 5–10 minutes, making sure all sides are toasted.

TO ASSEMBLE THE CAKE
Trim the three sponges and soak the tops with vanilla syrup, according to the instructions given on pages 150–51.

Spread a layer of mango frosting over the first sponge, then place the second sponge on top. Spread the second sponge with a thin layer of frosting, followed by some of the jelly and another thin layer of frosting. Add the final sponge layer.

Mask the top and sides of the cake with the remaining mango frosting. For full instructions, see pages 152–53.

TO DECORATE
Top the cake with the remaining passion fruit jelly. If the jelly cracks as you transfer it to the cake, you can smooth it using a blowtorch. Press the toasted coconut shavings around the sides of the cake.

If stored in the fridge, this cake will last for up to 5 days; however it tastes best if consumed within 3 days. Serve at room temperature.

CHOCOLATE PRALINE TRUFFLE CAKE

THIS CAKE IS A SHOW STOPPER, PERFECT FOR CHOCOLATE LOVERS. IT LOOKS IMPRESSIVE, YET IT IS RELATIVELY EASY TO MAKE. THE DESIGN LENDS ITSELF TO ALL SORTS OF OCCASIONS, SUCH AS BIRTHDAYS, WEDDINGS AND ANNIVERSARIES.

INGREDIENTS

For the chocolate cake
300g butter
1kg light brown sugar
300g plain chocolate drops (53% cocoa solids)
450ml milk
9 medium eggs, beaten
675g plain flour
6¾ tablespoons cocoa powder
2¼ teaspoons bicarbonate of soda
2¼ teaspoons baking powder
½ teaspoon salt

For the chocolate ganache
1kg plain Belgian chocolate drops
(53% cocoa solids)
750ml whipping cream
100g glucose

For the meringue buttercream
270g caster sugar
67ml water
135g egg whites, fresh or pasteurised
330g butter, softened

For the praline filling
600g chocolate ganache
750g meringue buttercream
150g caster sugar
300g hazelnuts, toasted

For the decoration
3–4kg (300–400) praline chocolate truffles

EQUIPMENT

baking tool kit (see page 8)
layering tool kit (see page 8)
three 15cm and three 20cm round sandwich tins
baking tray
small food processor or blender
4 cake dowels
one 15cm and one 20cm round cake card

Makes one 15cm and one 20cm round cake tier,
serving 60 finger slices or 30 dessert portions.

METHOD

Make the chocolate cake one day ahead.

TO MAKE THE CHOCOLATE CAKE

Preheat the oven to 160°C/gas mark 3.

Line three 15cm and three 20cm sandwich tins with oil spray and greaseproof paper.

Place the butter and half the brown sugar in an electric mixer and, using the paddle, beat at medium-high speed until pale and fluffy.

Meanwhile, place the chocolate drops, milk and remaining sugar in a deep pan and bring to the boil, stirring occasionally. When the butter and sugar mixture has turned pale and fluffy, slowly add the eggs.

Sift together the flour, cocoa powder, bicarbonate of soda, baking powder and salt and add to the mixture, with the mixer set on slow speed.

Pour the hot chocolate mixture into a jug and slowly pour it into the cake batter, still mixing on slow speed. Take care, as it could splash.

Once combined, pour the hot cake batter into the prepared tins. Bake for 20–30 minutes. The sponge is cooked when it springs back to the touch and the sides are starting to come away from the edges of the tin. If you insert a knife or wooden skewer, it should come out a bit sticky as the texture should be slightly gooey.

Once cooked, let the cakes rest in the tin for about 10 minutes, then transfer to a wire rack to cool.

Wrap the sponges in cling film and leave to rest overnight at room temperature. This will ensure that all the moisture is sealed and the sponges are a good firm texture for trimming and layering.

TO MAKE THE PRALINE FILLING

Make the chocolate ganache following the instructions on page 13 (using the amounts given on page 76), then leave to cool to room temperature.

Make the meringue buttercream following the instructions on page 10 and leave to cool to room temperature.

Put the sugar in a saucepan over a medium heat and stir gently until caramelized.

Place the toasted hazelnuts on a lined baking tray. Pour the caramelized sugar over the top and leave to cool and set. Smash the praline into pieces, then grind in a food processor until the texture resembles rough sand.

Gently fold 600g ganache into 750g buttercream and combine well. Take care not to overwork the mixture as it can split. Fold through the praline.

TO ASSEMBLE THE CAKE

Trim the six sponge layers and sandwich together using the praline filling, so you have one 15cm cake and one 20cm cake. See pages 150–51 for instructions on how to trim and layer the cakes.

Place each cake on a turntable and, using the remaining ganache, mask the top and sides of the cakes (see pages 152–53). Chill until set.

Trim the 4 cake dowels so they are the same height as the 20cm cake, and push them into the cake in a square formation, as close to the outside as possible but so that they will fit underneath the top tier.

Spread a little ganache in the middle and centre the 15cm cake tier on top.

TO DECORATE THE CAKE

Using a large step palette knife, transfer the cake to a cake stand or serving platter. If you are transporting the cake to a venue, place it on a cake drum that is at least 8cm larger than the bottom tier.

Trim each truffle to make a flat surface. Pour the remaining ganache into a piping bag and use it to stick the truffles onto the cake (the flattened side should sit against the cake). Start by making a row around the bottom and work your way up. (See overleaf, pictures 1–4.) Should the ganache be too firm to pipe, warm it in a microwave until soft but not runny.

Store the cake in the fridge if not serving immediately. Serve at room temperature. Keep away from heat and direct sunlight. The cake tastes best if consumed within 3 days of baking, but will last for up to 1 week if stored in the fridge.

MAPLE AND WALNUT CAKE

THIS IS A LOVELY SUBTLE CAKE WITH A DENSE NUTTY TEXTURE, ABSORBING THE
OOZY MAPLE SYRUP PERFECTLY. THE TREE-TRUNK BUTTERCREAM DECORATION
PROVIDES A QUIRKY RUSTIC TWIST. ADD MARZIPAN LEAVES AND ACORNS
TO COMPLETE THE LOOK.

INGREDIENTS

For the walnut sponge
4 eggs
150g icing sugar
150g butter, melted
120ml milk
175g plain flour
1 tablespoon baking powder
a pinch of salt
125g ground almonds
100g walnuts, toasted and finely chopped

For the maple sugar syrup
150ml water
150g sugar
100ml maple syrup

For the maple frosting
250g full-fat cream cheese, slightly softened
250g unsalted butter, softened
625g icing sugar, sifted
4 tablespoons dark maple syrup

For the decoration
Acorns and maple leaves made from marzipan

EQUIPMENT

baking tool kit (see page 8)
layering tool kit (see page 8)
three 15cm round sandwich tins
side scraper with a fine comb patterned edge

Makes one 15cm round cake, serving 8 generous slices.

METHOD

Make the sponge one day ahead.

TO MAKE THE WALNUT SPONGE

Preheat the oven to 175°C/gas mark 4.

Line three 15cm sandwich tins with oil spray and greaseproof paper.

Place the eggs and icing sugar in an electric mixer and, using the paddle, beat at medium-high speed until pale and fluffy.

Add the butter and milk, beating at medium speed.

In a separate bowl, sift the flour, baking powder and salt, then fold into the mixture.

Fold in the almonds and walnuts, then transfer the batter to the lined tins.

Bake for 20–25 minutes. The sponge is cooked when it springs back to the touch and the sides are coming away from the edges of the tin. If you insert a clean knife into the centre, it should come out clean.

While the sponges are baking, make the sugar syrup following the instructions on page 13 and adding the maple syrup.

When the sponges are baked, remove from the oven and leave them to rest for about 10 minutes. Brush the tops of the sponges with maple sugar syrup (reserving some for the assembling stage and storing it in the fridge overnight).

Once just warm, run a knife all the way round the sides of the tins, remove the sponges and leave to cool completely on a wire rack.

Wrap the cooled sponges in cling film and leave to rest overnight at room temperature. This will ensure that all the moisture is sealed and the sponges firm up to the perfect texture for trimming and layering.

TO MAKE THE MAPLE FROSTING

Make some cream-cheese frosting following the instructions on page 12.

Gently fold in the maple syrup, then refrigerate for at least 2 hours, or until set.

TO ASSEMBLE THE CAKE

Trim the three sponge layers and soak the tops with more maple sugar syrup. Sandwich the layers together using the maple frosting. See pages 150–51 for instructions on trimming and layering your cake.

Mask the top and sides of the cake with the remaining maple frosting (see pages 152–53).

TO DECORATE

While the final layer of frosting is still soft, using a side scraper with a fine patterned edge, scrape the sides of the cake in a vertical motion all around to create a tree-trunk effect.

To mark the top, gently push the tip of a palette knife into the middle of the cake and slowly spin the turntable. Gradually move the palette knife towards the outside as you spin, until you reach the edge.

Decorate the cake with marzipan acorns and leaves, and serve with maple syrup.

If stored in the fridge, this cake has a shelf life of up to 5 days; however, it tastes best if consumed within 3 days of baking. Serve at room temperature.

TIRAMISU CAKE

THIS IS A DELICIOUS AFTER-DINNER CAKE OR BIRTHDAY CAKE FOR GENTS. IT LOOKS ATTRACTIVE INSIDE AND OUT, AS IT REVEALS THE LAYERS OF COFFEE, BUTTERCREAM AND SPONGE WHEN YOU SLICE INTO IT.

INGREDIENTS

For the coffee sponge

600g salted butter
600g caster sugar
1 tablespoon vanilla extract
12 medium eggs, room temperature
600g self-raising flour, sifted
2 tablespoons espresso or strong instant coffee

For the coffee syrup

250ml water
250g caster sugar
100ml espresso or strong instant coffee
Marsala liqueur, to taste

For the mascarpone frosting

100g unsalted butter, softened
250g icing sugar, sifted
150g mascarpone, slightly softened

For the coffee buttercream

500g unsalted butter, softened
500g icing sugar, sifted
a pinch of salt
1 tablespoon espresso or strong instant coffee

For the decoration

About 3 tablespoons cocoa powder
coffee buttercream
12–16 chocolate coffee beans

EQUIPMENT

baking tool kit (see page 8)
layering tool kit (see page 8)
three 25cm round sandwich tins
ridged side scraper
piping bag
medium star piping nozzle

Makes one 25cm cake, serving 12–16 generous slices.

METHOD

Make the sponge one day ahead.

TO MAKE THE COFFEE SPONGE

Preheat the oven to 175°C/gas mark 4.

Line three 25cm sandwich tins with oil spray and greaseproof paper.

Place the butter, caster sugar and vanilla in an electric mixer and, using the paddle, beat at medium-high speed until pale and fluffy.

Lightly beat the eggs in a separate bowl or jug and, with the mixer set on medium speed, slowly pour the eggs into the mixture. If it starts to curdle, add a tablespoon of flour to bring it back together.

Once the butter, sugar and eggs are combined, add the flour and espresso, mixing at low speed, until it is just incorporated.

Using the rubber spatula, fold through the batter to make sure everything is well combined.

Transfer the batter to the lined tins and gently spread it towards the edges with a step palette knife. The mixture should be higher around the edges of the tin than in the centre, to ensure an even the cake bakes evenly and the height is level.

Bake for 25–30 minutes. The sponge is cooked when it springs back to the touch and the sides are coming away from the edges of the tin. If you insert a clean knife into the middle of the sponge, it should come out clean.

While the sponges are baking, make the sugar syrup as shown on page 13 and flavour with the espresso or instant coffee. Once cool, add the liqueur to taste.

When the sponges are baked, remove from the oven and leave them to rest for about 10 minutes. Brush the tops of the sponges with coffee syrup (reserving some for the assembling stage and storing it in the fridge overnight).

Once just warm, run a knife all the way round the sides of the tins, remove the sponges and leave to cool completely on a wire rack.

Wrap the cooled sponges in cling film and leave to rest overnight at room temperature. This will ensure that all the moisture is sealed so the sponges firm up to the perfect texture for trimming and layering.

TO MAKE THE MASCARPONE FROSTING

Follow the instructions on page 12 using the amounts on page 86 and chill until set.

TO MAKE THE COFFEE BUTTERCREAM

Follow the instructions for English buttercream on page 10, using the amounts on page 86. Gently fold in the coffee and mix well. Allow to chill until set.

TO ASSEMBLE THE CAKE

Trim the three sponge layers and soak the tops with more coffee syrup. Spread mascarpone frosting over each layer and dust with cocoa powder before placing the next sponge on top. For instructions on trimming and layering your cake, see pages 150–51.

Mask the top and sides of the cake with coffee buttercream (see pages 152–53).

TO DECORATE

Place the cake on a turntable.

Cover the chilled cake with another generous layer of buttercream and, using a ridged side scraper, create a sculptured barrel design (see overleaf, steps 1–2).

Chill the cake again until set (about 1 hour).

Dust the top of the cake liberally with cocoa powder (step 3).

Make a two-tone buttercream by mixing 1 tablespoon of coffee buttercream with 1 teaspoon of cocoa powder. Spread a thin line around the inside of the piping bag (step 4), then fill the bag with the remaining lighter coffee buttercream (steps 5–7).

Pipe small rosettes around the top of the cake (steps 8–9) and top each one with a chocolate coffee bean.

Store the cake in the fridge if not serving immediately and serve at room temperature. This cake tastes best if consumed within 3 days of baking, but will last for up to 1 week if stored in the fridge.

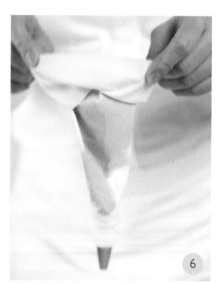

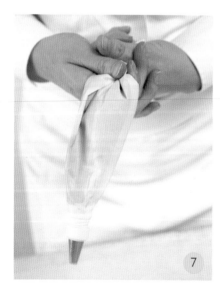

CITRUS CAKE

THIS IS A REFRESHING SUMMERY PARTY CAKE BASED ON A SIMPLE VICTORIA SPONGE. YOU CAN COMBINE ANY CITRUS ZESTS – I USED LIME, LEMON AND ORANGE FOR MY SPONGE AND PINK GRAPEFRUIT TO FLAVOUR THE FROSTING. I FIND THIS BITTERSWEET AND ZESTY COMBINATION PARTICULAR TASTY.

INGREDIENTS

For the citrus sponge
400g butter
400g caster sugar
finely grated zest of 2 oranges, 2 lemons
and 2 limes (reserve the juice for the syrup)
8 medium eggs, room temperature
400g self-raising flour, sifted

For the citrus syrup
200g caster sugar
juice of 2 oranges, 2 lemons and 2 limes

For the pink-grapefruit frosting
375g full-fat cream cheese, slightly softened
375g unsalted butter, softened
950g icing sugar, sifted
zest of 2 unwaxed pink grapefruits
peach food paste colour

For the buttercream decoration
300g butter
300g icing sugar
peach, yellow and green food paste colour

EQUIPMENT

baking tool kit (see page 8)
layering tool kit (see page 8)
three 20cm round sandwich tins
fine grater
3 piping bags
3 large open star piping nozzles
(You could get away with using just one
nozzle and piping bag, but it will take a bit
longer as you will need to wash them
between each use)

Makes one 20cm cake, serving 12 generous slices.

METHOD

Make the sponge one day ahead.

TO MAKE THE CITRUS SPONGE

Preheat the oven to 175°C/gas mark 4.

Line three 20cm sandwich tins with oil spray and greaseproof paper.

Place the butter, caster sugar and orange, lemon and lime zests in an electric mixer and, using the paddle, beat at medium-high speed until pale and fluffy.

Lightly beat the eggs in a separate bowl or jug and, with the mixer set at medium speed, slowly pour into the butter mixture. If it starts to curdle, add a tablespoon of flour to bring it back together.

Once the butter, sugar and eggs are combined, mix the flour at low speed until it is just incorporated.

Using a rubber spatula, fold through the batter to make sure everything is well combined.

Transfer the batter to the lined tins and gently spread it towards the edges with a step palette knife. The mixture should be higher around the edges than in the centre, to ensure the cake bakes evenly and the height is level.

Bake for 20–25 minutes. The sponge is cooked when it springs back to the touch and the sides are coming away from the edges of the tin. Alternatively, insert a clean knife into the middle of the sponge; if it is cooked, the knife will come out clean.

While the cake is baking, make the citrus syrup. Put the sugar and citrus juices in a medium saucepan, bring to the boil, then leave to cool.

Once the sponges are baked, remove from the oven and leave to rest for about 10 minutes. Brush the tops of the sponges with citrus syrup (reserving some for the assembling stage and storing it in the fridge overnight).

Run a knife all the way round the sides of the tins, remove the sponges and leave to cool completely on a wire rack.

Once cool, wrap the sponges in cling film and leave to rest overnight at room temperature. This will ensure that all the moisture is sealed and the sponges firm up to the perfect texture for trimming and layering.

TO MAKE THE PINK-GRAPEFRUIT FROSTING

Make some cream-cheese frosting following the instructions on page 12, using the amounts given on page 92 and including the pink-grapefruit zest.

Add a little peach food colour to a little frosting, mixing until the colour is well incorporated. Stir into the remaining frosting to make a pale peach shade.

Refrigerate until the frosting has set.

TO ASSEMBLE THE CAKE

Trim the three sponge layers and soak the tops with citrus syrup. Sandwich together using the pink-grapefruit frosting. See pages 150–51 for trimming and layering instructions.

Mask the top and sides of the cake with the remaining pink grapefruit frosting (see pages 152–53).

TO DECORATE

Cream together the butter and icing sugar to make a buttercream, following the instructions for English buttercream on page 10.

Divide the buttercream between 3 small bowls and mix each part with a different food colour, so you have pale shades of yellow, peach and lime green.

Put each batch of buttercream into a piping bag with a star nozzle attachment. (If you only have one bag and nozzle, wash them between each colour and start with the palest.)

Pipe stars of different sizes and colours randomly over the top of the cake. For a detailed view of the nozzle and piping style, see page 155.

Store the cake in the fridge if not serving immediately, and serve at room temperature. Keep away from heat and direct sunlight. This cake tastes best if consumed within 3 days of baking, but can last for up to 1 week if stored in the fridge.

BERRY BASKET CAKE

THIS IS A DELICIOUSLY LIGHT CAKE, BURSTING WITH BERRY FLAVOURS. YOU CAN KEEP THE DECORATION SIMPLE OR PIPE THE SIDES OF THE CAKE WITH BASKET WEAVE. THE HEXAGON SHAPE IS A LITTLE CHALLENGING, BUT YOU COULD MAKE A ROUND CAKE IF YOU PREFER, USING THE QUANTITIES GIVEN HERE.

INGREDIENTS

For the chiffon sponge
320g egg yolks
900g caster sugar
300ml vegetable or sunflower oil
660g egg whites
a pinch of cream of tartar
a pinch of salt
2½ tablespoons vanilla extract
900g plain flour
60g baking powder
480g milk

For the vanilla syrup
250ml water
250g caster sugar
2 tablespoons vanilla extract

For the meringue buttercream
1.1kg caster sugar
268ml water
540g egg whites
1.3kg butter
vanilla extract, to taste

For the filling
1 medium-sized jar raspberry jam
1 medium-sized jar blueberry jam
about 2 punnets each of fresh raspberries,
blueberries and blackberries
about 1 punnet of strawberries

For the decoration
fresh berries and flowers (make sure they are
suitable for direct food contact, i.e. not
poisonous or treated with pesticides)

EQUIPMENT

baking tool kit (see page 8)
layering tool kit (see page 8)
two 15cm and two 25cm hexagon cake tins
one 15cm and one 25cm hexagon cake card
4 cake dowels
piping bag
round piping nozzle no. 3
medium basket weave piping nozzle
open star piping nozzle no. 7

Makes one 15cm and one 25cm hexagon cake tier,
serving about 30 dessert portions or 80 finger portions.

METHOD

Make the sponge one day ahead.

TO MAKE THE CHIFFON SPONGE

Preheat the oven to 175°C/gas mark 4.

Line the cake tins with oil spray and greaseproof paper.

Whisk the egg yolks with a little of the sugar until pale and fluffy. Slowly add the oil and whisk until thick.

Put the egg whites, cream of tartar and salt in an electric mixer and, using the whisk attachment, beat at medium-high speed until the mixture forms soft peaks.

With the mixer still running, slowly pour in the remaining sugar and beat until the mixture is glossy and holds stiff peaks. Beat in the vanilla extract.

In a medium-sized bowl, sift together the flour and baking powder and gradually add to the egg-yolk mixture, gently folding after each addition. Add the milk and fold in the stiff egg whites.

Transfer the batter to the lined tins and gently spread it towards the edges with a step palette knife. The mixture should be higher around the edges than in the middle, to ensure an even bake and level cake height.

Bake for 25–30 minutes. The sponges are cooked when they spring back to the touch and the sides are coming away from the edges of the tin.

While the sponges are baking, make the sugar syrup following the instructions on page 13, using the amounts on page 96, and add vanilla extract to taste.

When the sponges are baked, remove from the oven and leave them to rest for about 10 minutes. Brush the tops of the sponges with vanilla syrup (reserving some for the assembling stage and storing it in the fridge overnight).

Transfer the sponges to a wire rack to cool completely, then wrap them in cling film and rest overnight at room temperature.

TO MAKE THE MERINGUE BUTTERCREAM

Follow the instructions on page 10, using the amounts given on page 96, then add vanilla extract to taste.

TO ASSEMBLE THE CAKE

Trim the sponges and slice each one in half horizontally, so you have 4 layers for each tier. Soak each sponge layer with vanilla syrup, then spread the fillings on top, using raspberry jam for the first layer, meringue buttercream and fresh berries for the second and blueberry jam for the third. See pages 150–51 for trimming and layering instructions.

Mask the top and sides of the cake with the remaining meringue buttercream. (See pages 152–53.) Keep the corners as sharp and straight as possible.

Trim the 4 dowels to the same height as the bottom tier and push them into the centre of the cake in a square formation. They should be as far apart as possible, but within the diameter of the tier above.

Spread more buttercream between the dowels and centre the second tier on top. Pipe buttercream into the gap between the tiers, then run your finger along the edge to give it a smooth finish.

TO DECORATE

Place the cake on a turntable with a 30cm cake disc. Put the remaining meringue buttercream in a piping bag fitted with the round nozzle.

Starting with the top tier, pipe vertical lines down each side of the cake, first in the middle, then on the corners, then at 1cm intervals in between.

Fit the piping bag with the basket weave nozzle and, starting at the bottom, pipe a row of strips over every other line. Repeat on the next row, working in between the strips on the first row.

Once the cake is covered with the basket weave effect, attach the star nozzle to the piping bag and pipe a scroll border along the top edge of each tier. (See page 155 for detailed images of these piping effects.)

Refrigerate for about 1 hour, then transfer the cake to a serving platter or cake stand using a large step palette knife. Arrange fresh berries and flowers in two clusters on the top and side of the cake.

If stored in the fridge, this cake will last for up to 3 days. Serve at room temperature.

GINGERBREAD CAKE

THIS IS A FANTASTIC CAKE TO SHARE WITH FAMILY AND FRIENDS DURING THE FESTIVE SEASON. IT IS LOVELY AND SPICY AND IS TOPPED WITH SCRUMPTIOUS LEMON FROSTING. I DECORATE MINE WITH CUTE LITTLE GINGERBREAD MEN, BUT YOU CAN USE ANY COOKIE SHAPES – THIS CAKE INVITES YOU TO BE CREATIVE AND HAVE FUN.

INGREDIENTS

For the sponge
about 250ml whole milk
finely grated zest and juice of 1 unwaxed orange
150g dark muscovado sugar
a pinch of salt
300g golden syrup
150g dark treacle
4 teaspoons ground ginger
4 teaspoons ground cinnamon
2 teaspoons ground allspice
180g unsalted butter, chilled and cut into pieces
350g self-raising flour
1 teaspoon bicarbonate of soda
3 medium eggs, beaten

For the sugar syrup
150ml water
150g caster sugar

For the lemon cream-cheese frosting
250g full-fat cream cheese, slightly softened
250g unsalted butter, softened
625g icing sugar, sifted
finely grated zest of 2 unwaxed lemons

For the decoration
about 8 gingerbread men (you can buy these or make your own)
a little royal icing (if making your own gingerbread)

EQUIPMENT

baking tool kit (see page 8)
layering tool kit (see page 8)
three 15cm round sandwich tins
small gingerbread cookie cutter (if making your own gingerbread)
paper piping bag (if decorating your own gingerbread)
piping bag
medium round piping nozzle

Makes one 15cm round cake, serving 8 generous slices.

METHOD

Make the sponge one day ahead.

TO MAKE THE GINGERBREAD SPONGE
Preheat the oven to 175°C/gas mark 4.

Line three 15cm sandwich tins with oil spray and greaseproof paper.

Add enough milk to the orange juice to make up 300ml of liquid. Place the milk mixture in a saucepan with the zest, sugar, salt, golden syrup, treacle and spices and gently bring to the boil, stirring constantly.

Remove from the heat and add the butter, stirring with a whisk until melted.

Sift the flour and bicarbonate of soda into a large bowl and add the slightly cooled liquid mixture. Stir gently with a whisk.

Gradually add the beaten egg and stir through until the cake batter is just smooth and thoroughly combined.

Pour the mixture into a jug, then transfer to the prepared tins.

Bake for 25–30 minutes. The sponge is cooked when it springs back to the touch and the sides are coming away from the edges of the tin. If you insert a clean knife into the middle of the sponge, it should come out clean.

While the sponges are in the oven, make the sugar syrup following the instructions on page 13.

Once the sponges are baked, remove from the oven and leave them to rest for about 10 minutes. Brush the tops of the sponges with sugar syrup.

Once just warm, run a knife all the way round the sides of the tins, transfer the sponges to a wire rack and leave to cool completely.

Once cool, wrap the sponges in cling film and leave them to rest overnight at room temperature. This will ensure that all the moisture is sealed and the sponges are a good firm texture for trimming and layering.

TO MAKE THE LEMON FROSTING
Make some cream-cheese frosting following the instructions on page 12, then add the lemon zest.

Chill for at least 2 hours, or until set.

TO ASSEMBLE THE CAKE
Trim the three sponge layers, then sandwich them together using lemon frosting. See pages 150–51 for instructions on trimming and layering your cake.

Mask the top and sides of the cake with lemon frosting (see pages 152–53).

TO DECORATE THE CAKE
If you have made your own gingerbread men, fill a paper piping bag with royal icing, snip off the tip to make a small hole, then pipe on faces and buttons.

Put the remaining lemon frosting into a piping bag with a medium round nozzle attached and pipe 8 blobs of frosting evenly around the edge of the cake.

Place a gingerbread man on top of each blob, facing towards the centre of the cake.

This cake has a shelf life of up to 1 week if stored in the fridge. Serve at room temperature.

SUGAR PLUM CAKE

THIS DELICIOUS AUTUMNAL CAKE IS SMARTLY DECORATED WITH OMBRÉ BUTTERCREAM STRIPES AND TOPPED WITH A CROWN OF GOLDEN PLUMS.

INGREDIENTS

For the cinnamon sponge
200g butter
200g caster sugar
1 teaspoon vanilla extract
4 medium eggs
200g self-raising flour, sifted
1 teaspoon ground cinnamon
a pinch of salt

For the cinnamon syrup
150ml water
150g caster sugar
1 cinnamon stick

For the filling
200g plum jam

For the cinnamon buttercream
500g unsalted butter, softened
500g icing sugar, sifted
a pinch of salt
1 tablespoon ground cinnamon, sifted
a little purple and pink food paste colour

For the decoration
2 fresh plums, pitted and quartered

EQUIPMENT

baking tool kit (see page 8)
layering tool kit (see page 8)
three 15cm round sandwich tins
3 petal piping nozzles (I used Wilton 104)
3 piping bags
(You can get away with just one nozzle and piping bag,
but it will take a bit longer as you need to wash them
between each use)
medium round piping nozzle

Makes one 15cm cake, serving 8 generous slices.

METHOD

Make the sponge one day ahead.

TO MAKE THE CINNAMON SPONGE

Preheat the oven to 175°C/gas mark 4 and line the sandwich tins with oil spray and greaseproof paper.

Place the butter, caster sugar and vanilla in an electric mixer and, using the paddle, beat at medium-high speed until pale and fluffy.

Lightly beat the eggs in a separate bowl or jug and, with the mixer set at medium speed, slowly pour into the butter mixture. If it starts to curdle, add a tablespoon of flour to bring it back together.

Sift together the flour, cinnamon and salt, add to the mixture and beat at low speed until just combined. Using a rubber spatula, fold through the batter to make sure everything is well combined.

Transfer the mixture to the lined tins and gently spread towards the edges with a step palette knife. The batter should be higher around the edges of the tins than in the centre, to ensure an even bake and level cake height.

Bake for 20–25 minutes. The sponges are cooked when they spring back to the touch and the sides are coming away from the edges of the tin. If you insert a clean knife into the middle of the sponge, it should come out clean.

While the sponges are baking, make the cinnamon sugar syrup following the instructions on page 13. When luke warm, add the cinnamon stick. Remove once the syrup has cooled.

When the sponges are baked, remove from the oven and leave to rest for about 10 minutes. Brush the tops with cinnamon syrup (reserving some for the assembling stage and storing it in the fridge overnight).

Once just warm, run a knife all the way round the sides of the tins, transfer the sponges to a wire rack and leave to cool completely.

Wrap the cooled sponges in cling film and rest overnight at room temperature. This will seal in all the moisture and ensure that the sponges are a good firm texture for trimming and layering.

TO MAKE THE CINNAMON BUTTERCREAM

Make some English buttercream following the instructions on page 10, using the amounts given on page 105. Add the cinnamon and purple food colour and mix to a light shade of purple.

TO ASSEMBLE THE CAKE

Trim the three sponge layers and soak the tops with more cinnamon syrup. Sandwich together using the plum jam. See pages 150–51 for instructions on trimming and layering the cake.

Place the cake on a turntable and mask the top and sides with the purple buttercream (see pages 152–53). Apply two layers, or until there is no crumb visible. Chill until set.

TO DECORATE

Divide the remaining buttercream evenly between 3 bowls. Keep one batch in its original colour (the middle shade), then add more purple to the second batch to make it darker and a small amount of pink to the third to make it lighter.

Put each batch of buttercream into a piping bag with a petal nozzle attached. (If you only have one bag and nozzle, start with the darkest shade and wash them before adding the middle shade.)

Apply the darkest buttercream first, piping 3–4 rows around the bottom of the cake, then repeat with the middle then lightest shade, moving up the sides. You should end up with three even stripes of buttercream around the cake. (See overleaf, steps 1–2.)

Use the side scraper to smooth the buttercream, rotating the turntable as you work. You should end up with an ombré effect (see steps 3–4).

Put the remaining dark purple buttercream in a piping bag fitted with a round nozzle and pipe 8 swirls evenly around the top of the cake. Top each swirl with a fresh plum quarter.

Store in the fridge if not serving immediately and serve at room temperature. Keep away from heat or direct sunlight. This cake tastes best if consumed within 3 days of baking, but lasts for up to 1 week if stored in the fridge.

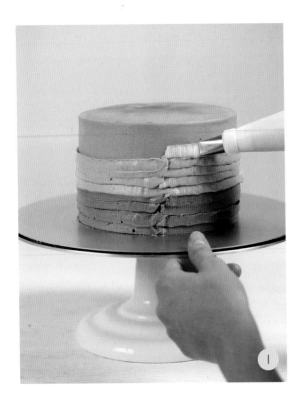
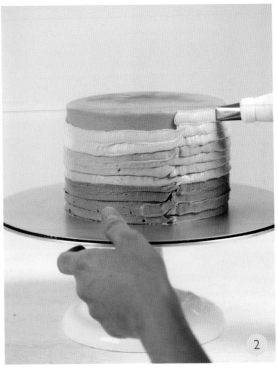
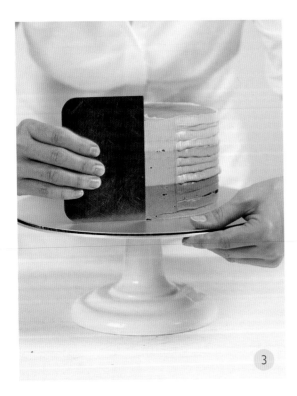

SPICED PUMPKIN CAKE

THIS IS A GREAT CAKE FOR THE AUTUMN SEASON, PERFECT TO CELEBRATE THANKSGIVING OR HALLOWEEN. IT HAS A MOIST AND DENSE TEXTURE YET IT TASTES LIGHT, CREAMY AND SPICY. I MADE MY OWN PUMPKIN DECORATIONS FROM MARZIPAN, BUT YOU COULD BUY THESE.

INGREDIENTS

For the pumpkin sponge

100g butter
280g pumpkin purée
½ teaspoon fine sea salt
115g buttermilk
325g light brown sugar
4 eggs
240g plain flour
2½ teaspoons baking powder
½ teaspoon bicarbonate of soda
¾ teaspoon ground ginger
1 teaspoon ground cinnamon
¾ teaspoon ground nutmeg
¼ teaspoon ground cloves

For the cinnamon frosting

250g full-fat cream cheese, slightly softened
250g unsalted butter, softened
625g icing sugar, sifted
1 tablespoon ground cinnamon

For the decoration

marzipan pumpkins (bought or homemade)

EQUIPMENT

baking tool kit (see page 8)
layering tool kit (see page 8)
three 15cm round sandwich tins
patterned side scraper

Makes one 15cm cake, serving 8 generous portions.

METHOD

Make the sponge one day ahead.

TO MAKE THE PUMPKIN SPONGE
Preheat the oven to 170°C/gas mark 3.

Line three 15cm round sandwich tins with oil spray and greaseproof paper.

Melt the butter and leave to cool slightly. Put the pumpkin purée, salt, buttermilk and sugar in the large bowl of an electric mixer and, using the whisk attachment, mix well.

Add the eggs gradually, whisking well between each addition.

Sift together the flour, baking powder, bicarbonate of soda and spices. Lightly whisk the flour mix into the pumpkin mixture in two batches. Add the melted butter and gently incorporate until just mixed.

Carefully pour the mixture into the prepared cake tins and bake for 20–25 minutes or until the sponges spring back when gently prodded and an inserted skewer comes out clean.

Remove the cakes from the oven and leave to rest for about 10 minutes. Once just warm, run a knife all the way round the sides of the tins, remove the sponges and leave to cool completely on a wire rack.

Wrap the sponges in cling film and leave them to rest overnight at room temperature. This will ensure that all the moisture is sealed and the sponges firm up to the perfect texture for trimming and layering.

TO MAKE THE CINNAMON FROSTING
Make some cream-cheese frosting following the instructions on page 12.

Gently fold in the ground cinnamon and chill for at least 2 hours, or until set.

TO ASSEMBLE THE CAKE
Trim the three sponge layers and sandwich them together using the cinnamon frosting. (See pages 150–51 for instructions on trimming and layering your cake.)

Mask the top and sides of the cake with the remaining cinnamon frosting (see pages 152–53).

TO DECORATE
Mask the chilled cake again, using a generous layer of cinnamon frosting. Use a side scraper with a patterned edge to go around the sides of the cake. See the Tiramisu Cake on pages 86–91 for a similar method, with detailed images.

Chill again until set.

Decorate the top of the cake with marzipan pumpkins.

NEAPOLITAN CAKE

THIS IS A DELICIOUS COMBINATION OF LIGHT CHIFFON SPONGE AND SMOOTH CHOCOLATE MERINGUE BUTTERCREAM. CHIFFON SPONGE NATURALLY HAS A VERY LIGHT COLOUR AND LENDS ITSELF PERFECTLY TO THE CREATION OF THESE DIFFERENT SHADES, WHICH ARE CURRENTLY SO POPULAR.

INGREDIENTS

For the chiffon sponge
160g egg yolks
450g caster sugar
150ml vegetable oil
330g egg whites
a pinch of cream of tartar
a pinch of salt
3 tablespoons vanilla extract
450g plain flour
30g baking powder
240g milk
15g cocoa powder, sifted
a little pink food colour

For the vanilla syrup
250ml water
250g caster sugar
2 tablespoons vanilla extract

For the meringue buttercream
540g caster sugar
134ml water
270g egg whites
660g butter

For the chocolate ganache
400g Plain Belgian chocolate drops
(53% cocoa solids)
300ml whipping cream
40g glucose

For the decoration
cocoa powder
plain meringue buttercream

EQUIPMENT

baking tool kit (see page 8)
layering tool kit (see page 8)
three 20cm round sandwich tins
polka dot cake stencil
piping bag
large round piping nozzle

Makes one 20cm round cake, serving 12–16 generous slices.

METHOD

Make the sponge one day ahead.

TO MAKE THE CHIFFON SPONGES
Preheat the oven to 175°C/gas mark 4.

Line three 20cm sandwich tins with oil spray and greaseproof paper.

Place the egg yolks and a little of the sugar in an electric mixer and, using the whisk attachment, beat until pale and fluffy. Add the oil slowly and mix well until thick.

Put the egg whites, cream of tartar and salt in an electric mixer and, again using the whisk attachment, beat at medium-high speed until the mixture forms soft peaks.

With the mixer still running, slowly pour in the remaining sugar and beat until the mixture is glossy and holds stiff peaks. Beat in the vanilla extract.

Sift the flour and baking powder together into a medium-sized bowl.

Gradually add the flour mixture to the egg-yolk mixture, gently folding after each addition to incorporate. Add the milk and fold in the stiff egg whites.

Gently divide the mixture evenly between 3 bowls. Fold the cocoa powder into one batch and the pink food colour into another. You should now have one plain mixture, one chocolate and one pink.

Transfer the batter to the lined tins and gently spread it towards the edges with a step palette knife. The mixture should be higher around the edges of the tin and lower in the centre.

Bake for 25–30 minutes. Insert a clean knife into the middle of each sponge; if they are cooked, the knife will come out clean.

While baking, make some sugar syrup following the instructions on page 13, using the amounts on page 114, then add the vanilla extract to taste.

When the sponges are baked, remove from the oven and leave them to rest for about 10 minutes. Brush the tops of the sponges with vanilla syrup (reserving some for the assembling stage and storing it in the fridge overnight).

Once the sponge is just warm, run a knife all the way round the sides of the tins, then transfer the sponges to a wire rack and leave to cool completely.

Wrap the sponges in cling film and leave to rest overnight at room temperature.

TO MAKE THE MERINGUE BUTTERCREAM
Follow the instructions on page 10, using the amounts on page 114. Leave to cool at room temperature.

TO MAKE THE CHOCOLATE GANACHE
Follow the instructions on page 13, using the amounts on page 114. Leave to cool at room temperature.

TO MAKE THE CHOCOLATE BUTTERCREAM
Reserve about 250g of the buttercream for the decoration. Gently fold 700g chocolate ganache into 1kg 150g meringue buttercream, being careful not to overwork as it can split.

TO ASSEMBLE THE CAKE
Trim the sponges and soak with more vanilla syrup. Sandwich the sponges together, with the chocolate at the bottom, the pink in the middle and the vanilla on the top. Spread a coating of chocolate buttercream between each layer. See pages 150–51 for trimming and layering instructions.

Mask the top and the sides of the cake with the remaining chocolate buttercream (see pages 152–53).

TO DECORATE THE CAKE
Centre the polka dot stencil on the top of the chilled cake and dust liberally with the cocoa powder. Carefully remove the stencil.

Put the remaining plain meringue buttercream in a piping bag fitted with a large round nozzle and pipe 12 blobs evenly around the outside of the cake.

If stored in the fridge, this cake will last for up to 5 days; however, it tastes best if consumed within 3 days of baking. Serve at room temperature.

BLACK FOREST CAKE

DERIVED FROM MY GERMAN HERITAGE, THIS IS A SUMPTUOUS AND BOOZY TAKE ON
THE TRADITIONAL 'SCHWARZWÄLDER KIRSCHTORTE'. I USE GRIOTTINE CHERRIES
(MORELLO CHERRIES MARINATED IN KIRSCH LIQUEUR), BUT IF YOU CAN'T FIND THEM
YOU CAN SOAK YOUR OWN MORELLO CHERRIES FOR A COUPLE OF DAYS BEFORE USE.

INGREDIENTS

For the chocolate sponge
100g butter
340g light brown sugar
100g plain chocolate drops (53% cocoa solids)
150ml milk
3 medium eggs
225g plain flour
2¼ tablespoons cocoa powder
¾ teaspoon bicarbonate of soda
¾ teaspoon baking powder
a pinch of salt
griottine cherries, drained (reserve the
syrup for soaking)

For the Kirsch frosting
250g full-fat cream cheese, slightly softened
250g unsalted butter, softened
625g icing sugar, sifted
1 tablespoon vanilla extract
4 tablespoons Kirsch liqueur (or to taste)

For the decoration
Kirsch frosting
griottine cherries
chocolate sprinkles

EQUIPMENT

baking tool kit (see page 8)
layering tool kit (see page 8)
three 15cm round sandwich tins
piping bag
medium star piping nozzle

Makes one 15cm round cake, serving 8 generous slices.

METHOD

Make the sponge one day ahead.

TO MAKE THE CHOCOLATE SPONGE

Preheat the oven to 160°C/gas mark 3.

Line three 15cm sandwich tins with oil spray and greaseproof paper.

Place the butter and half the sugar in an electric mixer and, using the paddle attachment, beat at medium-high speed until pale and fluffy.

Meanwhile, put the chocolate, milk and remaining sugar in a deep saucepan and bring to the boil, stirring occasionally.

When the butter and sugar is pale and fluffy, slowly add the eggs.

Sift together the flour, cocoa powder, bicarbonate of soda, baking powder and salt and add to the mixture while beating at slow speed.

Pour the hot chocolate mixture into a jug and slowly pour it into the cake batter while mixing on slow speed. Take care, as the hot mixture could splash.

Once combined, pour the hot cake batter into the prepared tins. Drop a handful of the cherries into each tin.

Bake for 20–25 minutes. The sponge is cooked when it springs back to the touch and the sides are coming away from the edges of the tin. If you insert a clean knife into the middle of the sponge, it should NOT come out clean but with a small amount of crumb. Be careful not to overbake this cake; it should have a slightly gooey texture.

Once cooked, let the cakes rest for about 10 minutes. Brush the tops with the syrup reserved from the griottine cherries, allow to cool until just warm and then transfer to a wire rack and leave to cool completely.

Wrap the sponges in cling film and leave them to rest overnight at room temperature. This will ensure that all the moisture is sealed and the sponges firm up to the perfect texture for trimming and layering.

TO MAKE THE KIRSCH FROSTING

Make some cream-cheese frosting following the instructions on page 12.

Gently fold through the vanilla extract and Kirsch liqueur to taste.

Chill in the fridge until set.

TO ASSEMBLE THE CAKE

Trim the three sponge layers and soak the tops with more of the reserved griottine cherry syrup. Sandwich together using Kirsch frosting, and scatter a handful of griottine cherries evenly over the frosting before placing the next sponge layer on top. See pages 150–51 for instructions on how to trim and layer your cake.

Place the cake on a turntable and mask with Kirsch frosting (see pages 152–53).

TO DECORATE

Fill a piping bag with the remaining Kirsch frosting and, using a star nozzle, pipe 8 rosettes around the outside of the cake.

Top each rosette with a griottine cherry and lightly sprinkle the cake with chocolate.

Store the cake in the fridge if not serving immediately. Serve at room temperature. Keep away from heat and direct sunlight. This cake tastes best if consumed within 3 days of baking, but can last for up to 1 week if stored in the fridge.

CHEEKY MONKEY CAKE

THIS IS A YUMMY, WHOLESOME CAKE, LOVED NOT ONLY BY CHILDREN BUT BY GROWN-UPS, TOO. IF YOU PREFER NOT TO DECORATE IT WITH SWEETS, USE FRESH BANANA SLICES INSTEAD.

INGREDIENTS

For the banana sponge
225g butter
450g light brown sugar
1 teaspoon vanilla extract
3 eggs
600g overripe banana, mashed
150g chocolate chips, chopped
405g plain flour, sifted
9g bicarbonate of soda
9g white wine vinegar

For the vanilla syrup
150ml water
150g caster sugar
1 tablespoon vanilla extract

For the peanut buttercream
270g caster sugar
67ml water
135g egg whites
330g butter
4 tablespoons peanut butter, smooth

For the decoration
chocolate vermicelli
foam banana sweets

EQUIPMENT

baking tool kit (see page 8)
layering tool kit (see page 8)
three 15cm round cake tins
piping bag
large star piping nozzle

Makes one 15cm cake, serving 8 generous slices.

METHOD

Make the sponge one day ahead.

TO MAKE THE BANANA SPONGE

Preheat the oven to 175°C/gas mark 4.

Line three 15cm sandwich tins with oil spray and greaseproof paper.

Place the butter, light brown sugar and vanilla in an electric mixer and, using the paddle, beat at medium-high speed until pale and fluffy.

Lightly beat the eggs in a separate bowl or jug and slowly pour into the butter mixture while paddling on medium speed. If it starts to curdle, add a tablespoon of flour to bring it back together.

Once the butter, sugar and eggs are combined, add the mashed banana and chocolate chips and beat at low speed until just combined.

Add the flour using the rubber spatula, folding through the batter to make sure everything is well combined.

Mix together the bicarbonate of soda and white wine vinegar and quickly add to the mixture.

Transfer the batter to the lined tins and gently spread it towards the edges with a step palette knife. Bake for 20–25 minutes.

The sponge is cooked when it springs back to the touch and the sides are coming away from the edges of the tin. If you insert a clean knife into the middle of the sponge, it should come out clean.

While the sponges are in the oven, cook the sugar syrup following the instructions on page 13. Add the vanilla extract.

Remove the sponges from the oven and leave them to rest for about 10 minutes. Brush the tops of the sponges with vanilla syrup (reserving some for the assembling stage and storing it in the fridge overnight).

Once just warm, run a knife all the way round the sides of the tins, remove the sponges and leave to cool completely on a wire rack.

Wrap the sponges in cling film and leave to rest overnight at room temperature. This will ensure that all the moisture is sealed and the sponges firm up to the perfect texture for trimming and layering.

TO MAKE THE PEANUT MERINGUE BUTTERCREAM

Make some meringue buttercream following the instructions on page 10.

Gently fold the peanut butter into 750g meringue buttercream.

TO ASSEMBLE THE CAKE

Trim the three sponge layers and soak the tops with vanilla syrup. Sandwich together using the peanut buttercream. See pages 150–51 for trimming and layering instructions.

Mask the top and sides of the cake with peanut buttercream (see pages 152–3).

TO DECORATE

Sprinkle plenty of chocolate vermicelli onto a baking tray lined with greaseproof paper.

Roll the sides of the chilled cake over the vermicelli, so that you have an even covering. If you prefer, you can apply the sprinkles by hand, holding the cake at an angle.

Fill a piping bag with the remaining peanut meringue buttercream and, using a star nozzle, pipe upside-down shell scrolls onto the top of the cake. Top each scroll with a banana sweet.

If stored in the fridge, this cake will last for up to 5 days; however, it tastes best if consumed within 3 days of baking. Serve at room temperature.

STRAWBERRY AND CHAMPAGNE CAKE

THIS IS A DELECTABLE CAKE, PERFECT FOR A ROMANTIC CELEBRATION. THE GOLD DRAGÉES ADD A TOUCH OF GLAMOUR, BUT YOU COULD USE FRESH STRAWBERRIES OR CHAMPAGNE CHOCOLATE TRUFFLES INSTEAD.

INGREDIENTS

For the vanilla sponge
800g butter
800g caster sugar
1 tablespoon vanilla extract
16 medium eggs
800g self-raising flour, sifted

For the champagne syrup
500ml water
500g caster sugar
4 tablespoons Marc de champagne
(add to taste)

For the English buttercream
1kg unsalted butter, softened
1kg icing sugar, sifted
½ teaspoon salt
a little pink food paste colour

For the filling
600g strawberry & champagne preserve

For the decoration
gold dragées

EQUIPMENT

baking tool kit (see page 8)
layering tool kit (see page 8)
three 10cm, three 15cm and three 20cm
round sandwich tins
one 10cm, one 15cm and one 20cm
round cake card
5 cake dowels
piping bag

Makes one 10cm, one 15cm and one 20cm round cake tier.
Serves about 70 finger portions or about 25 dessert slices.

METHOD

Make the sponge one day ahead.

TO MAKE THE VANILLA SPONGES
Preheat the oven to 175°C/gas mark 4.

Line all the sandwich tins with oil spray and greaseproof paper.

Place the butter, caster sugar and vanilla in an electric mixer and, using the paddle, beat at medium-high speed until pale and fluffy.

Lightly beat the eggs in a separate bowl or jug and, with the mixer set at medium speed, slowly pour into the butter mixture. If it starts to curdle, add a tablespoon of flour to bring it back together.

Once the butter, sugar and eggs are combined, add the flour and mix at low speed until just incorporated. Using the rubber spatula, fold through the batter to make sure everything is well combined.

Transfer the batter to the lined tins and gently spread it towards the edges with a step palette knife. The mixture should be higher around the edges than in the middle, to ensure an even bake and level top.

Bake for 20–30 minutes. The sponge is cooked when it springs back to the touch and the sides are coming away from the edges of the tin. If you insert a clean knife into the centre, it should come out clean.

While the cake is baking, make the sugar syrup following the instructions on page 13, using the amounts given on page 126. Leave to cool, then add the Marc de Champagne to taste.

Remove the sponges from the oven and leave to rest for about 10 minutes. Brush the tops of the sponges with champagne syrup (reserving some for the assembling stage and storing it in the fridge overnight).

Once just warm, remove the sponges from the tins and leave to cool completely on a wire rack.

Wrap the sponges in cling film and leave to rest overnight at room temperature. This will seal in all the moisture and ensure that the sponges firm up to the perfect texture for trimming and layering.

TO MAKE THE ENGLISH BUTTERCREAM
Make English buttercream following the instructions on page 10, using the amounts given on page 126. Mix in enough pink food colour to make a pale peachy pink.

TO ASSEMBLE THE CAKE
Trim the sponge cakes and soak the tops with champagne syrup, then sandwich the layers together using the strawberry and champagne preserve (see pages 150–51 for trimming and layering tips). You should end up with one 10cm cake, one 15cm cake and one 20cm cake, all of the same height.

Place each cake on a turntable and mask with pink buttercream (see pages 152–53 for instructions on masking the cakes).

Trim 4 cake dowels to the same height as the 20cm cake tier and 1 dowel to the same height as the 15cm tier (check against the correct tier, just in case there is a slight variation).

Take the 4 trimmed dowels and push them into the centre of the 20cm tier in a square formation, as close to the outside as possible without going beyond the circumference of the tier that will sit above. Push the single dowel into the centre of the 15cm tier.

Spread a small amount of buttercream around the middle of the 20cm tier and centre the 15cm cake on top. Repeat the process on the 15cm tier and place the 10cm cake on top. Make sure that all three tiers are perfectly centred and level.

Put some buttercream in a paper piping bag, snip off the tip and use it to fill any gaps between the tiers. Use your little finger to smooth the buttercream and create a neat finish.

TO DECORATE
Pipe a little buttercream onto the gold dragées and stick them around the base of each tier in a random champagne-bubble pattern.

Store the cake in the fridge if not serving immediately and serve at room temperature. Keep away from heat or direct sunlight. The cake tastes best if consumed within 3 days of baking, but will last for up to 1 week if stored in the fridge.

S'MORES CAKE

●●

INSPIRED BY THE AMERICAN CAMPFIRE TREAT, THIS CAKE IS MADE FROM A LIGHTLY
SPICED SPONGE, DRENCHED IN HONEY SYRUP, LAYERED WITH CHOCOLATE GANACHE
AND BUTTERCREAM AND FINISHED WITH BURNED MERINGUE.

INGREDIENTS

For the spiced sponge
105g butter
275g light brown sugar
1 teaspoon vanilla extract
2 eggs
250g plain flour
1 teaspoon ground cinnamon
a pinch of salt
250g buttermilk
1¼ teaspoons white wine vinegar
1 teaspoon bicarbonate of soda

For the honey syrup
125ml water
125ml honey

For the meringue buttercream
270g caster sugar
67ml water
135g egg whites
330g butter

For the Italian meringue
112g sugar
45ml water
2 egg whites
a pinch of cream of tartar
a pinch of salt

For the chocolate ganache
200g plain Belgian chocolate drops
(53% cocoa solids)
150ml whipping cream
20g glucose

EQUIPMENT

baking tool kit (see page 8)
layering tool kit (see page 8)
three 15cm shallow round sandwich tins
sugar thermometer
side scraper
piping bag
large round piping nozzle
blowtorch

Makes one 15cm round cake, serving 8 generous slices.

METHOD

Make the sponge one day ahead.

TO MAKE THE SPICED SPONGE

Preheat the oven to 175°C/gas mark 4.

Line the three sandwich tins with oil spray and greaseproof paper.

Place the butter, sugar and vanilla in the bowl of an electric mixer fitted with the paddle, then beat at medium-high speed until pale and fluffy.

Lightly beat the eggs in a separate bowl or jug and, with the mixer set at medium speed, slowly pour into the butter mixture. If the mixture starts to curdle, add a tablespoon of flour to bring it back together.

Sift the flour, cinnamon and salt into a bowl. Mixing at low speed, gently add these dry ingredients and the buttermilk in batches.

Mix together the vinegar and bicarbonate of soda and quickly add to the mixture. Using a rubber spatula, gently fold through the mixture to make sure there are no lumps.

Transfer the batter to the tins and gently spread out towards the edges with a step palette knife. Bake for 20–25 minutes. The sponge is cooked when it springs back to touch and the sides are coming away from the edges of the tin.

While the sponges are baking, make the honey syrup. Heat the water and honey in a saucepan, stirring regularly, until the honey has dissolved.

Remove the sponges from the oven and leave them to rest for about 10 minutes. Using a pastry brush, soak the tops with the honey syrup.

Remove the sponges from the tins and leave to cool completely on a wire rack.

Wrap the sponges in cling film and leave to rest overnight at room temperature.

TO MAKE THE MERINGUE BUTTERCREAM

Make the meringue buttercream following the instructions on page 10.

TO MAKE THE ITALIAN MERINGUE

Put the sugar and water in a small saucepan over a medium-high heat and bring to the boil.

Place the egg whites, cream of tartar and salt in an electric mixer and, using the whisk attachment, whip at a low speed until frothy.

When the sugar mixture reaches a rapid boil, check the temperature and cook until it reaches 121°C.

With the mixer running, pour the syrup directly over the meringue in a thin, steady stream, avoiding the whisk and the sides of the bowl. Whip until cool to the touch; this could take a few minutes. The meringue should be shiny and stiff (see overleaf, step 1). Leave to cool completely.

TO MAKE THE CHOCOLATE GANACHE

Please follow the instructions on page 13.

TO ASSEMBLE THE CAKE

Trim the sponges and soak the tops with more of the honey syrup. Sandwich the sponges together, spreading an even coating of chocolate ganache and a layer of buttercream in between the layers. See pages 150–51 for a step-by-step guide to trimming and layering your cake.

Crumb coat the top and sides of the cake (see pages 152–53) with the remaining meringue buttercream and chill until set.

TO DECORATE

For the final mask, cover the top and sides of the cake with Italian meringue using a palette knife (see overleaf, steps 2–3), then use a side scraper to create a smooth finish around the sides (step 4) and the palette knife to level off the top (step 5).

Put the remaining meringue in a piping bag fitted with a large round nozzle. Pipe 'flames' onto the top of the cake (steps 6–7).

Using a blowtorch, lightly brown the sides and the top of the cake (steps 8–9).

If stored in the fridge, this cake will last for up to 3 days. Serve at room temperature.

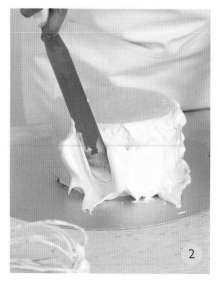

MAD HATTER'S CHECKERBOARD CAKE

THIS CAKE IS SO INTRIGUING – ALL YOUR GUESTS WILL WONDER HOW YOU CREATED THIS STRIKING CHECKERBOARD PATTERN.

INGREDIENTS

For the vanilla sponge
200g unsalted butter
200g caster sugar
1 tablespoon vanilla extract
4 medium eggs, room temperature
200g self-raising flour, sifted

For the chocolate sponge
100g unsalted butter
340g light brown sugar
100g plain chocolate drops (53% cocoa solids)
150ml milk
3 medium eggs
225g plain flour, sifted
2¼ tablespoons cocoa powder
¾ teaspoon bicarbonate of soda
¾ teaspoon baking powder
a pinch of salt

For the vanilla syrup
150ml water
150g caster sugar
1 tablespoon vanilla extract (or to taste)

For the buttercream
300g unsalted butter, softened
300g icing sugar, sifted
a pinch of salt
1 tablespoon vanilla extract

For the decorations
buttercream
Hydrangea design: green and purple food colour
Rosebud design: green and pink food colour
Blossom design: yellow food colour
silver sugar pearls

EQUIPMENT

baking tool kit (see page 8)
layering tool kit (see page 8)
four 15cm round sandwich tins
round pastry cutters, about 12cm, 9cm and 5cm in diameter
piping bag
small crimped star piping nozzle (hydrangea/rosebud)
small leaf piping nozzle (hydrangea/rosebud)
medium petal piping nozzle, Wilton 104 (blossom)

Makes one 15cm round cake, serving 8 generous slices.

METHOD

Make the sponge one day ahead.

TO MAKE THE VANILLA SPONGE

Preheat the oven to 175°C/gas mark 4 and line two sandwich tins with oil spray and greaseproof paper.

Put the butter, caster sugar and vanilla in an electric mixer and, using the paddle, beat at medium-high speed until pale and fluffy.

Lightly beat the eggs, then slowly pour into the mixer, beating at medium speed. If the mixture curdles, add a tablespoon of flour to bring it back together.

Once the butter, sugar and eggs are combined, add the flour and mix at low speed until just incorporated. Using a rubber spatula, fold through the batter to make sure everything is well combined. Transfer the batter to the lined tins, then bake for 20–25 minutes.

While the sponges are baking, make the sugar syrup following the instructions on page 13, using the amounts given on page 136 and adding the vanilla.

Remove the sponges from the oven and leave to rest for 10 minutes. Using a pastry brush, soak the tops with vanilla syrup, then transfer to a wire rack to cool completely. Wrap the sponges in cling film and leave to rest overnight at room temperature.

TO MAKE THE CHOCOLATE SPONGE

Preheat the oven to 160°C/gas mark 3 and line two sandwich tins with oil spray and greaseproof paper.

Put the butter and half of the brown sugar in an electric mixer and, using the paddle attachment, beat at medium-high speed until pale and fluffy.

Meanwhile, put the chocolate, milk and remaining sugar in a deep pan and bring to the boil, stirring occasionally.

Slowly add the eggs to the butter mixture. Sift together the flour, cocoa powder, bicarbonate of soda, baking powder and salt. Add to the mixture, beating slowly.

Transfer the hot chocolate mixture to a jug and slowly pour into the cake batter while mixing at slow speed. Once combined, pour the hot cake batter into the prepared tins and bake for 20–25 minutes.

When the sponges are baked, remove from the oven and allow to cool and rest as for the vanilla sponges.

TO MAKE THE BUTTERCREAM

Make the English buttercream following the instructions on page 10, using the amounts given on page 136. Fold in the vanilla once the basic ingredients are combined.

TO ASSEMBLE THE PURPLE CAKE

Trim the sponges as shown on pages 150–51, step 1.

Using the pastry cutters, cut each sponge into even rings (see opposite, steps 1–2). Alternate the flavours of the cut-outs and stick the rings together using a thin layer of piped buttercream (steps 3–7).

Sandwich the layers with a thin coating of buttercream (step 8), making sure you alternate the colours (step 9).

Put a small amount of buttercream in a bowl, add a little green food colour and mix to a light green.

Mask the top and sides of the cake with buttercream, as shown on pages 152–53. Combine the remaining buttercream with a little purple food colour to achieve a light purple, and use for the final layer of masking. For the pink or yellow cake, adjust the colour accordingly.

TO DECORATE THE PURPLE CAKE

Divide the remaining purple buttercream between two bowls. Add more purple food colour to one bowl.

Put the lighter shade into a piping bag and, using the star nozzle, pipe small, well-spaced hydrangea blossoms in clusters on the top and sides of the cake. Pipe darker purple blossoms in between the paler ones.

Put the green buttercream into a piping bag fitted with the leaf nozzle and pipe leaves around the clusters.

For detailed images of the piping effects used on the cakes shown on pages 138–39, see page 154. To recreate the yellow blossoms, pipe the buttercream onto small squares of greaseproof paper, holding the nozzle rounded side downwards in the middle of the paper. As you squeeze the piping bag, move the nozzle back and forth, working around until you have a full blossom. Press a sugar pearl into the centre. Chill until set, then press onto the cake.

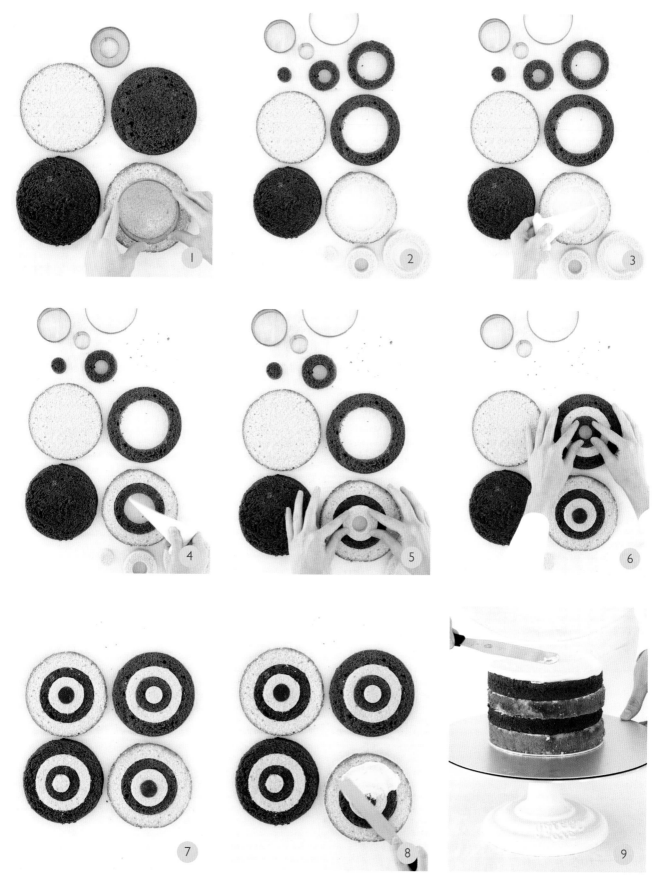

MAD HATTER'S CHECKERBOARD CAKE

PEACH AND ALMOND TORTE

THIS CAKE IS BASED ON A RECIPE FOR ONE OF THE VERY FIRST LAYER CAKES THAT I ATTEMPTED AS A TEENAGER. IT'S A DELICATE ALMOND SPONGE SOAKED WITH GRAND MARNIER SYRUP AND LAYERED WITH CINNAMON BUTTERCREAM AND POACHED PEACHES.

INGREDIENTS

For the almond sponge

200g salted butter
200g caster sugar
1 teaspoon vanilla extract
4 medium eggs, room temperature
200g self-raising flour, sifted
100g ground almonds

For the poached peaches

200ml water
200g caster sugar
2 cinnamon sticks
3 fresh peaches, peeled

For the Grand Marnier syrup:

strained poaching liquid
Grand Marnier, to taste

For the cinnamon meringue buttercream

540g caster sugar
134ml water
270g egg whites
660g butter
2 tablespoons ground cinnamon, to taste

For the decoration

8 golden sugared almonds
marzipan peaches (bought or homemade)

EQUIPMENT

baking tool kit (see page 8)
layering tool kit (see page 8)
three 15cm round sandwich tins
piping bag
round piping nozzle no. 3
For the tiered cake only: 8 cake dowels
one 15cm, one 20cm and one 25cm round cake card

Makes a 15cm round cake, serving 8 generous slices.
To recreate the 3-tier cake shown, you will need a 25cm, 20cm and 15cm tier.
Multiply the amounts by three for a 25cm tier and by two for a 20cm tier.

METHOD

Poach the peaches and make the sponge one day ahead of the cake.

TO POACH THE PEACHES

Put the water, sugar and cinnamon sticks in a medium-sized saucepan and bring to a simmer.

Put the peaches in the liquid and poach gently for about 15–20 minutes, until tender but not soft. Turn the peaches around during poaching and frequently baste with the syrup. Remove from the poaching liquid and leave to cool.

Bring the poaching liquid to the boil and reduce by half, then add the Grand Marnier according to taste.

TO MAKE THE ALMOND SPONGE

Preheat the oven to 175°C/gas mark 4.

Line three sandwich tins with oil spray and greaseproof paper.

Put the butter, caster sugar and vanilla in an electric mixer and, using the paddle, beat at medium-high speed until pale and fluffy.

Lightly beat the eggs and, with the mixer set at medium speed, slowly add to the mixture. If it starts to curdle, add a tablespoon of flour.

Once the butter, sugar and eggs are combined, add the flour and ground almonds and beat at low speed until just incorporated. Using a rubber spatula, fold through the batter to make sure everything is mixed well.

Transfer the batter to the lined tins and gently spread towards the edges with a step palette knife. Bake for 20–25 minutes.

When the sponges are baked, remove from the oven and leave to rest for about 10 minutes. Brush the tops of the sponges with Grand Marnier syrup (reserving some for the assembling stage and storing it in the fridge overnight).

Remove the sponges from the tins and leave to cool completely on a wire rack. Then, wrap the sponges in cling film and leave to rest overnight at room temperature.

TO MAKE THE CINNAMON MERINGUE BUTTERCREAM

Make the meringue buttercream following the instructions on page 10, using the amounts given on page 143. Add the ground cinnamon to taste.

TO ASSEMBLE THE CAKE

Slice each peach in half, remove the stone and cut into thin, even slices.

Trim the sponge layers and soak with Grand Marnier syrup. Spread a thin layer of cinnamon meringue buttercream over each sponge, then arrange peach slices evenly on top, making sure the surface is completely covered. Spread another thin layer of buttercream over the peaches before placing the next sponge layer on top. For trimming and layering instructions, see pages 150–51.

Mask the top and sides of the cake with the cinnamon meringue buttercream (see pages 152–53).

TO DECORATE

Put the remaining meringue buttercream in a piping bag fitted with the round nozzle. Pipe a snail trail around the base of the cake. Pipe a row of double swags around the top edge of the cake and place a sugared almond over each join. For detailed images of the piping techniques used here, see page 154.

Decorate the top of the cake with marzipan peaches.

If not serving immediately, store the cake in the fridge where it will last for up to 5 days; however, it will taste best if consumed within 3 days of baking. Serve at room temperature.

FOR THE TIERED CAKE

Before you decorate the cake tiers, you will need to dowel and stack them. You will need 4 cake dowels for the bottom tier and 4 for the middle tier. They will prevent the cakes from sinking into each other. Cut the dowels to the same height as the tier and push them into the middle in a square formation, as far apart as possible but not beyond the circumference of the tier that will sit above. Stick the tiers in place using buttercream, and decorate as above.

PIÑA COLADA CAKE

THIS FABULOUS PARTY CAKE IS INSPIRED BY ONE OF MY FAVOURITE COCKTAILS. THE FRAGRANT AROMAS OF COCONUT, FRESH LIME ZEST AND PINEAPPLE EVOKE MEMORIES OF HOT SUMMER HOLIDAYS AT THE BEACH.

INGREDIENTS

For the pineapple flowers
1 fresh pineapple

For the coconut and pineapple sponge
225g butter
225g caster sugar
zest of 2 unwaxed limes
4 eggs
240g self-raising flour
100g desiccated coconut
150g fresh pineapple, cubed
(reserved from pineapple flowers)

For the malibu syrup
150ml water
150g caster sugar
Malibu liqueur, to taste

For the lime frosting
250g full-fat cream cheese, softened slightly
250g unsalted butter, softened
625g icing sugar, sifted
zest of 2 unwaxed limes
2 tablespoon Malibu liqueur

EQUIPMENT

baking tool kit (see page 8)
layering tool kit (see page 8)
long carving knife
paper towels
three 15cm shallow round sandwich tins
silicone tray with sphere moulds (see Suppliers on page 156)

Makes one 15cm cake, serving 20 slices.

METHOD

Make the pineapple flowers and sponge one day ahead (make the pineapple flowers first, so you can use the leftover pineapple for the sponge). Assemble the cake on the day.

TO MAKE THE PINEAPPLE FLOWERS

Place the pineapple on a chopping board and cut off the top and bottom. Carefully cut away the skin.

Using a long carving knife, cut waves lengthways around the sides of the pineapple to form a flower shape.

Slice the pineapple thinly, so you have at least 15 flowers. Dab the flowers with a paper towel to help them to dry out. Place them in a sphere tray, then put them in the oven at 110°C/gas mark ¼ for a few hours, until dried out. They should hold their shape.

Leave the flowers to cool, then immediately wrap them in cling film to keep them crisp.

TO MAKE THE COCONUT AND PINEAPPLE SPONGE

Preheat the oven to 175°C/gas mark 4.

Line three 15cm sandwich tins with oil spray and greaseproof paper.

Place the butter, caster sugar and lime zest in an electric mixer and, using the paddle, beat at medium-high speed until pale and fluffy.

Lightly beat the eggs in a separate bowl or jug and, with the mixer set at medium speed, slowly pour into the butter mixture. If it starts to curdle, add a tablespoon of flour to bring it back together.

Once the butter, sugar and eggs are combined, add the flour, coconut and pineapple.

Transfer the batter to the lined tins and gently spread towards the edges with a step palette knife. The mixture should be higher around the edges than in the middle, to ensure an even bake and level height.

Bake for 20–25 minutes. The sponge is cooked when it springs back to the touch and the sides are coming away from the edges of the tin. A clean knife inserted into the centre of the sponge should come out clean. While the sponges are in the oven, make some sugar syrup following the instructions on page 13. Leave to cool, then add the Malibu liqueur according to taste.

When the sponges are baked, remove from the oven and leave to rest for about 10 minutes. Brush the tops of the sponges with Malibu syrup (reserving some for the assembling stage and storing it in the fridge overnight).

Run a knife all the way round the sides of the tins, remove the sponges and leave to cool completely on a wire rack.

Wrap the sponges in cling film and leave to rest overnight at room temperature. This will ensure that all the moisture is sealed and the sponges firm up to the perfect texture for trimming and layering.

TO MAKE THE LIME FROSTING

Make some cream-cheese frosting following the instructions on page 12, then fold in the lime zest and Malibu liqueur.

TO ASSEMBLE THE CAKE

Trim the three sponge layers and soak with Malibu syrup, then sandwich together using the lime frosting. See pages 150–51 for instructions on how to trim and layer the cake.

Mask the top and sides of the cake with lime frosting, following the instructions on pages 152–53.

TO DECORATE

Just before serving, arrange the pineapple flowers on the top of the cake, attaching them with dabs of cream-cheese frosting. Note that, once exposed to air, the flowers will start to soften and begin to lose their shape.

If stored in the fridge, this cake will last for up to 5 days; however, it will taste best if consumed within 3 days of baking. Serve at room temperature.

LAYERING TECHNIQUE

THESE INSTRUCTIONS ARE A GENERAL GUIDE TO TRIMMING AND LAYERING; THE PROCESS WILL VARY SLIGHTLY FROM ONE RECIPE TO ANOTHER. MAKE SURE ALL THE SPONGE LAYERS HAVE COOLED COMPLETELY BEFORE ASSEMBLING. IDEALLY, WRAP THEM IN CLING FILM AND LEAVE TO REST OVERNIGHT. ANY BUTTERCREAM, GANACHE OR OTHER FILLINGS SHOULD BE SPREADABLE. ENSURE THAT THEY ARE ROOM TEMPERATURE BEFORE USE.

1 Using a bread knife or cake leveller, trim the top crust off each sponge. For the middle layer (or layers), also trim off the browned base of the sponge. Aim to make all the sponges the same depth – to help with this, I use a ruler when adjusting my cake leveller. After trimming, brush the crumbs off the sponge cakes, as they can make masking very difficult and spoil the filling.

2 Stick a cake board in the centre of the cake disc using buttercream or ganache, then place the disc on a non-slip turntable (optional). Spread the cake board with a thin layer of buttercream or ganache and stick the first cake layer on top (brown side downwards). Use a pastry brush to soak the top of the sponge with sugar syrup, if required.

3 If the filling is different to that which will be used to coat the outside of the cake, put some of the outer coating mixture in a piping bag and pipe a ring around the edge of the layer. This will form a barrier to hold the filling inside.

4 Use a palette knife to spread the filling over the bottom layer.

5 Spread out the filling evenly, making sure it goes right to the edges (or meets the ring applied in step 3). Be careful not to use too much filling; if applied too heavily, the filling will ooze out around the sides when the next sponge layer is put in place.

6 Place the next sponge layer on top and add more sugar syrup if required.

7 Repeat steps 3–5. If your cake has more than three layers, repeat these steps until you just have the top layer left to add.

8 Position the final layer on top, brown side upwards.

9 Once all the layers are assembled, gently press on the top layer to release any trapped air bubbles. Make sure the top is level. Soak the final layer with sugar syrup if required.

MASKING TECHNIQUE

TO ACHIEVE A BEAUTIFULLY MASKED LAYER CAKE, IT IS IMPORTANT TO HAVE THE RIGHT EQUIPMENT (SEE PAGE 8). I ALSO RECOMMEND HAVING A DAMP CLOTH TO HAND, TO CLEAN THE EDGE OF YOUR PALETTE KNIFE AND SIDE SCRAPER AS YOU WORK. YOUR FROSTING SHOULD BE SPREADABLE AND LUMP FREE, AND ENSURE THAT IT IS AT ROOM TEMPERATURE BEFORE USE. YOU WILL NEED TO MASK ANY CAKE TWICE TO ACHIEVE A SMOOTH FINISH AND STRAIGHT EDGES; HOWEVER, YOU CAN REPEAT THE PROCESS UNTIL YOU ARE HAPPY WITH THE RESULT. DO BEAR IN MIND THAT YOU WILL NEED TO CHILL THE CAKE AFTER EACH COAT, TO SET THE FROSTING. USE A SEPARATE BOWL FOR THE CRUMB COAT, TO AVOID SPOILING THE FROSTING FOR THE FINAL COAT.

1 Begin by applying a crumb coat. This will hold the sponge surface in place and provide a good basic shape with which to work. Using a palette knife, pile a generous amount of buttercream or ganache onto the top layer of the cake.

2 Working from the centre, spread the mixture towards the edges of the cake and down the sides.

3 As you spread the mixture around the sides, work your palette knife in a backwards and forwards motion, rotating the turntable in the opposite direction to the way that you're spreading.

4 Ensure that the cake is completely covered and that there are no gaps around the sides.

5 Place the side scraper on the far side of the cake, with the long straight edge against the cake at a 45° angle and the bottom of the side scraper sitting flat on the disc. Place your spare hand on the disc and the turntable, as close to your other hand as possible.

6 Rotate the turntable against the direction of the side scraper, smoothing the frosting until your hands meet at the front.

7 If there are still a lot of cracks or gaps in the frosting, repeat the side-scraping process. Once you are happy with the coating, lift off the side scraper and then clean it with the palette knife.

8 Use a palette knife to make the top of the cake smooth and neaten the edges.

9 Use the side scraper and the palette knife to remove any excess mixture.

Leave the cake to chill in the fridge for at least half an hour, then repeat the crumb coat if necessary, until you are happy with the shape.

Chill the cake again, until it is set.

To apply the final coat, repeat steps 1–9 using a fresh, crumb-free batch of buttercream or ganache. Aim for a perfectly level top and straight sides with sharp edges, to achieve the best result.

When you are satisfied with the final coat, put the cake back in the fridge for about 1 hour, or until the buttercream or ganache has set. Then apply any finishing touches.

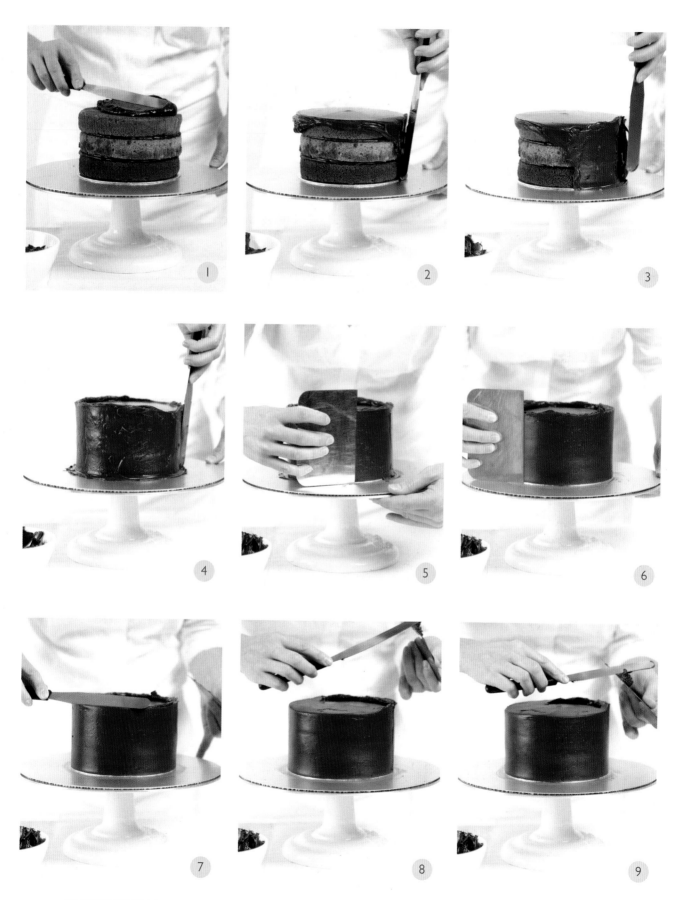

ROUND PIPING NOZZLE
NO. 3

CRIMPED STAR
NOZZLE

LOOP PIPING TECHNIQUE

SMALL LEAF
NOZZLE

SWAG PIPING TECHNIQUE

SNAIL TRAIL PIPING TECHNIQUE

HYDRANGEAS AND
LEAF TECHNIQUE

MEDIUM PETAL
NOZZLE

ROSE AND LEAF PIPING
TECHNIQUE

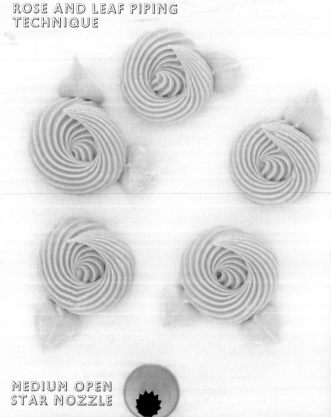

BLOSSOM PIPING
TECHNIQUE

MEDIUM OPEN
STAR NOZZLE

LARGE OPEN STAR
NOZZLE

MEDIUM OPEN
STAR NOZZLE

STAR PIPING
TECHNIQUE

ROSETTE PIPING
TECHNIQUE

ROUND PIPING
NOZZLE NO. 3

ROPE PIPING
TECHNIQUE

MEDIUM
BASKETWEAVE
NOZZLE

OPEN STAR
NOZZLE NO. 7

BASKET WEAVE PIPING
TECHNIQUE

INDEX

SUPPLIERS

MOST OF THE EQUIPMENT AND INGREDIENTS USED TO MAKE THE RECIPES IN THIS
BOOK ARE WIDELY AVAILABLE FROM SPECIALIST CAKE DECORATING SUPPLIERS AND,
INCREASINGLY, THE MORE EVERYDAY ITEMS CAN BE FOUND IN SUPERMARKETS AND
GENERAL COOKWARE SHOPS. HOWEVER, TO OFFER SOME GUIDANCE, AND TO HELP YOU
TO FIND THE MORE SPECIALIST ITEMS, I HAVE LISTED SOME USEFUL WEBSITES BELOW.

*My own website includes an online shop where
you can purchase specialist cake decorating
tools and ingredients as well as an assortment
of shallow sandwich tins, cake stencils and other
bakeware products. In addition, there is a small
selection of cake fillings:*
Peggy Porschen Cakes
www.peggyporschen.com

For cake tins:
Silverwood Quality Bakeware
www.alansilverwood.com

*For cake stencils, silicon moulds (such as
the insect mould for the Milk and Honey
Cake on page 22, made by First Impressions),
food colours and general baking and cake
decorating equipment:*
The Cake Decorating Co.
www.thecakedecoratingcompany.co.uk

For turntables:
Ateco
www.globalsugarart.com

Knightsbridge PME
www.cakedecoration.co.uk

For piping nozzles and patterned side scrapers:
Wilton
www.wilton.com

For specialist ingredients:
Whole Foods Market
www.wholefoodsmarket.com

*Throughout each year, I run a series of baking
and cake-decorating classes at the Peggy
Porschen Academy. So whether you want to
perfect your piping techniques to create irresistible
cakes or brush up your baking skills to make
heavenly cupcakes, there is a suitable course:*
Peggy Porschen Academy
30 Elizabeth Street
Belgravia
London SW1W 9RB
www.peggyporschen.com

*Each morning my team of specialist bakers freshly
bake a range of layer cakes, cupcakes, cookies
and other yummy delights for visitors to the Peggy
Porschen Parlour to either enjoy there and then
with an artisan tea blend or coffee or to take
away for a teatime treat. If you have enjoyed the
recipes in this book, I hope you will pay us a visit:*
Peggy Porschen Parlour
116 Ebury Street
Belgravia
London SW1W 9QQ
www.peggyporschen.com

ACKNOWLEDGEMENTS

Love Layer Cakes has been a labour of true love. An enormous amount of research, test baking, writing, photographing and more went into this book. I couldn't have done it without the help of a wonderful team of some very dedicated, talented people.

My first thank you goes to my long-term publisher Quadrille, with whom I have been working now for 10 fantastic years. I would especially like to thank Jane O'Shea, my publishing director. Thank you for 'discovering' me, for giving me all these amazing opportunities and for having shared my creative vision right from the start. I will miss working with you. To the other lovely ladies at Quadrille – Lisa Pendreigh, Helen Lewis and Gemma Hayden – thank you for everything and working so hard with me to add another beautiful title to the collection.

To my photographer, the one and only Georgia Glynn Smith, who goes above and beyond and produces the most beautiful pictures, every time. And to her assistant, Bobby – a huge, huge thank you to you both; it's been so much fun working with you at the shoots. Thank you to my lovely stylist Rebecca Newport, for all the beautiful props and setting the scene.

Probably the greatest thanks I owe to my fantastic staff member Michele Stander. Thank you so much for all your amazing help with the recipe testing and writing. You have put so much enthusiasm, talent and hard work into this book. You have made an incredible contribution and the result is a wonderful collection of deliciousness. I am very proud to have you in my team.

To Stephanie Maughan, thank you for your fantastic support, brainstorming ideas and help putting the concept together. Alexia Terzopulou, thank you for your editorial work. Another big thank you goes to the rest of my team at the Peggy Porschen Group. Whenever I am writing a book, it means a lot of extra work for everyone and disruption to their normal working day. I thank you guys for all your support and for keeping things going while Michele and I were producing this book.

Thank you to my neighbours and foodie friends Brian, Anke and Nicholas Ma Siy for tasting all our test cakes and giving your valuable feedback. I am so sorry for making you eat that much cake.

And to the most important people in my life, my little family. Bryn and Max, I love you both so, so much. My baby boy, Max, you made me so proud modelling for the Cheeky Monkey Cake.